Free the Unicorn

Hugh Gilbert

The Larry Czerwonka Company
Hilo, Hawaii

Copyright © 2013 by Hugh Gilbert

All rights reserved. No part of this book may be reproduced or transmitted in any form or by any means without written permission from the author.

Second Edition

Published by: The Larry Czerwonka Company
Printed in the United States of America

ISBN: 9798800210552

The Unicorn of Scotland stands chained to the throne in England's Coat of Arms. The symbolism is of the chaining of the hidden knowledge within all mankind that, if remembered, will return us to the all-powerful beings that we have forgotten that we are.

Cover design by Berangere Toulet

Contents

Introduction *1*

Prologue *3*

ONE

The "Law of Attraction" Was, on One Level, a Deliberate Deception!

The phrase "Law of Attraction" has created much frustration throughout Western society as millions of people globally have unsuccessfully attempted to implement it into their reality. This is not because it isn't a truth but is because we were consistently guided to narrow our focus onto the wrong aspect of it! *7*

TWO

The Day The Unicorn Was Born and Then Was Chained

Looking back, I realize now that my childhood dreams were indeed destined to come true as they are for each and every one of us. It is also painfully clear how my deliberate denial and repression of the truths that I could plainly see, and then acting out to fit the world as I was told I should, created a world of deep disconnection from my spirit, repeatedly manifesting for decades. If taken to heart, this chapter will prove to be life-changing for many readers. *11*

THREE

Mother/Child Connection . . . Uncovering the Miracle

The Mother/Child connection has been ignored by science throughout the ages. It is a very real energetic bond (predating science by millenia) with stunning potential as I initially discovered in Mexico and have had hundreds of validating experiences globally since. Mothers everywhere should read these true stories and reflect on them. *16*

FOUR

Mother Does Know Best!

There are so many heroines out there who are everyday mothers (often single Mothers) who are raising today's labelled children. In my experience, they are a vast source of untapped knowledge that needs to be heard. They often have to find solutions where the medical society has said there is none. I wish we could organise a conference to hear what they have to say. I know they hold many solutions for children everywhere. This is just one such story. *23*

FIVE

Our Narrow Focus is Our Prison!

When did you begin to focus on your shortcomings . . . and the perceived shortcomings of others? When were you indoctrinated into a tunnel vision view of yourself and others, and never genuinely allowed yourself to forgive others or to be forgiven? A Scottish Parable. *26*

SIX

The Young Guns of Patagonia

Today's young adults are truly here to make a difference in the world. They are all about integrity. They have many gifts (high intelligence, compassion, integrity, focus, psychically conscious, etc) that they bring to the table of life that are misunderstood and often deliberately repressed. I have had many incredible interactions with them globally, none more so than an afternoon in a bar in Patagonia. The palpable feeling of love I felt from them on that day has never left me. *31*

SEVEN

The "Law of Creation" Unfolds, and The Unicorn Remains in Chains and Darkness Within Me

Following my pivotal moment in childhood to deny the truth and to attempt to fit in to the world of the chicken coup as it appeared, the law of creation almost immediately and devastatingly reinforced my decision to see the world from my head and not my heart. This decision is one taken by millions of children globally, then and now, and is one which we need to prevent or reverse in ourselves or in others. *35*

EIGHT

A Telepathic and Clairvoyant Child, and Another, and Yet Another...

More miracles unfold as a non verbal child demonstrates her capabilities to me and to help others. There are millions of others just like her in the world, who have so much to offer, if only we would accept them just as they are and let them help us in ways we would consider miraculous, but to them are just natural. These kids certainly don't fit inside our concept of the chicken coup and are a beacon to a better way. *38*

NINE

Clearing the Land . . . Montana U.S.A.

The concept of clearing stuck or negative energy from land would have struck me as a strange and even bizarre concept in my early life. However, as I have come to understand the energetic principles involved it just makes sense. Now I am called intuitively and frequently by personal request to attend many sites throughout my Intercontinental Travels. Like doubting Thomas, I have always asked my God/Higher Power to give me proof that what I did or do was/is, in some way effective. This day, the miraculous proof was stunning and immediate, and I have the photographs to prove it to myself in case I ever doubt the glorious reality of the day at the Little Big Horn River in Montana U.S.A. *43*

TEN

Manifesting a Life of Denial and Separation

Just in case the episodes of trauma I had created were insufficient to keep me focussed on my perceived unworthiness, it was time for further, longer lasting methods of negative reinforcement. *52*

ELEVEN

Happy "Soul Soup" Stories

Church bells were ringing joyously. Masses and prayers were being offered. Street parties were spontaneously erupting. The following are all happy "soul soup" stories of how miracle status was given so many times, where it was in actuality quite explainable and, more importantly, teachable. *55*

TWELVE

Anyone Can Perform Miracles!

The beauty of my protocol KCR (Kinetic Chain Release) is that it can be learned by anyone and performed on family friends colleagues etc, with no previous medical knowledge required. Then the work I have been doing, often erroneously called miraculous, can be performed by anyone and achieve the same consistently stunning results on a whole array of medical conditions deemed as disability in Western Society. This is just one of the hundreds of incredible stories. *60*

THIRTEEN

ADD/ADHD/SOCIALLY INEPT/ or Simply an Easily Correctable Physical Restriction?

Another magical story from a Canadian mother of her 9 year old daughter's healing, which at one time would have been thought of as miraculous (and according to most western culture still would be) and yet, as you are now beginning to understand, the methodologies applied are simple, logical and sequential. There is nothing here that cannot be easily explained and, if you choose, can easily be learned. *62*

FOURTEEN

Finding My Way Home

Just what did it take to allow me not only to see where I had made the pivotal decision in my life, but to begin to repair the damage caused by that decision and to accept and manifest the truths I had known all along? *64*

FIFTEEN

Going Home to California (part one)

So much of our feelings of family dysfunction are often times nothing to do with the family. While our frustration at not being able to correct these dysfunctions can be very draining indeed, there are components which very much are within our grasp once we recognize them. *67*

SIXTEEN

Going Home to California (part two)

Turn your back on the land and you are turning your back on yourself! *70*

SEVENTEEN

Sticks and Stones . . .

Learn how this childhood mantra was yet another deliberate deception and see, in this simple story, just how quickly and easily its devastating effects on us all can be reversed. *73*

EIGHTEEN

Party Time! The Proof That Dreams DO Come True, and We DO Create!

How a simple relaxation exercise that I learned in a Management Course manifested in every tiny detail 5 years later. Because of this I had the tools to be free for the first time and could clearly see and finally celebrate that my childhood dreams of all of our unlimited human potential were correct. My "healing" had begun, however, if I only could have fully embraced that truth then it would all have resolved much faster. I know that by absorbing this story it will unlock the same potential in you, and that your acceptance of the facts can rocket you into the prosperity you seek. **78**

NINETEEN

"The Universe is in perfect order, the ONLY chaos is in our minds." ~ John F. Barnes, P.T.

The instant we realize this, then our journey becomes one of wonder and prosperity. I humbly relate the story of Laura's courage and her absolutely glittering miracle, in the knowing that it will assist all of you to release the chaos of your minds, created by "The Lies That Bind." **83**

TWENTY

The Power of Human Touch

We have forgotten the power of human touch. Many times it is all we need. "The Lies That Bind" have deliberately and relentlessly isolated our children (and you and I) from this most basic human need, and have deliberately created more chaos in our minds and increased the sense of separation in our hearts. Let the children of Sweden re-awaken this magic within you. **88**

TWENTY ONE

I Stopped Passing the Buck by Passing the Buck!

Each of us is capable of making massive changes to our world. It is all too easy to wring our hands and feel helpless to change things or to bury our heads in the sands of our selfishness and pretend all is well, regardless of how our action or lack of action impact others. This story is the proof of this and may be a motivator to some of you who could use a little confidence and direction for yourself to take action and make a difference in your world. ***92***

TWENTY TWO

"All the King's horses and all the King's men. Couldn't put Humpty together again."

There is an addendum to that nursery rhyme that has been erased from our consciousness: "But Humpty forgot that he could always rebuild himself!"

This is a true story of one man's global search for the best King's horses and men to help him, and how he was giving up hope until he found the answer in the one place he hadn't looked. The truth had always lain, hidden in plain sight, inside his own heart. Also, you will come to realize that abundance is NOT what you are seeking! The word itself deliberately sets you on the wrong path! ***98***

TWENTY THREE

Heroism is Not Spontaneous!

There have been several events in my life which have been deemed by some as somewhat heroic. I truly beg to differ. I believe with all my heart that there are certain times in our lives when, not by chance, we are placed to be of service to another. We appear, almost like angels, to interact briefly with another in trouble. We simply do what needs to be done without thinking. Take a moment now to remember when such spontaneous angels, usually strangers, appeared in your life, and also please accept and remember the times when, by a simple act of kindness you too became a spontaneous angel to another human being ***101***

TWENTY FOUR

Building Bridges TO the Children

Many are trying to build bridges FOR the labelled children to come into our conception of normality. Others attempt to force their cooperation and induction into compliance by medicating them with anti depressants etc. In some schools, in the USA, for example, over 70% of the male students are medicated! The Ties That Bind are desperately attempting to fit them into the chicken coup mentality. In my global travels, I have seen that the children are NOT the problem. They often bring solutions to a world in chaos. We need to build bridges TO them so we may cross over and learn from them. Many adults reading this are also just as gifted and just need the freedom to express themselves freely. ***109***

TWENTY FIVE

The Law of Creation

In Mexico, in just 24 hours I learned the Law of Creation through a stunningly simple formula which showed me that my resistance was indeed my only roadblock. ***113***

TWENTY SIX

Native American Vision Quest

Alone in the desert in Arizona, spending three days and two nights with no food and five liters of unusually warm drinking water, I was living out yet another boyhood dream. In the land of extreme heat and cold, cactus, rattlesnakes, scorpions, tarantulas and even mountain lions, I was experiencing a little of the trials and wonders of the Native American Vision Quest. It is a quest undertaken in different forms at some point by most of us. It is the search for answers as to who we truly are, and what our role in life truly is. "Hoka Hey"—it was a good day to die! **117**

TWENTY SEVEN

The Power of the Spoken Word

Let eight year old Chrissie's story teach you the power of the word "STOP." **124**

TWENTY EIGHT

6.9 Earthquake

Experiencing and surviving a 6.9 earthquake was a most unsettling experience and one which forever changes anyone who lives through it. However, the realizations we experienced later seemed much more surreal and difficult to explain, even to this day. **126**

TWENTY NINE

The Wheel Turns Full Cycle

I return to the land of my birth and of my perceived painful scenarios, where the healing had always been waiting for me. I allowed synchronicity and intuition to run my days unconditionally, and the outcomes were astounding. Being in this kind of flow should be the norm for us all; however, it is my hope that my story will inspire you to take the same approach to your life if only for a little while at first. ***130***

THIRTY

Doors Unlock, Mysteries Revealed, Others Take Their Place

Roslyn Chapel, Dan Brown, Knights Templar, Pirate Treasure, The Holy Grail. The stuff of myths and legends in the mists of time. I was about to be thrust head long into a life changing experience, the magic of which can still confuse me to this day. ***134***

THIRTY ONE

"Baggage" Return

You must become as sick of telling your story as we are of listening to it! That's the ugly truth. I have had clients who tell me that they have been everywhere trying to "heal" their issues. Even telling me they have travelled to Brazil to see John of God (a renowned healer) twice! If John of God couldn't do it in two tries, my chances are slim indeed!

Learn how to return these people's "baggage" to them and, as a by product release your own frustration. ***139***

THIRTY TWO

Energetically Drained

We have seen how other people can unload their negative energy on to us with devastating effect and discussed how not to accept it. However, another tragic component for many people is that they allow others to take their energy and leave them drained and vulnerable! How can you ever reach the prosperity you desire if you are constantly being energetically drained? It is crucial that we understand how to minimise this occurrence in a practical and logical manner and to teach our children to do the same. **143**

THIRTY THREE

Energetic Imprints

a) Lady Diana's resting place, b) The Factory in Mexico where a bloody revolution was born, and c) The Place of the Bones in Hawaii where a culture was almost destroyed. What did they have in common? Specific energetic imprints. Let me explain in this chapter.

To further help those of you who have always been sensitive to energy and spirits etc, and to raise awareness of the rest, here are some true experiences, which I hope will make life much easier for you and also help to settle the energy of the planet. **146**

THIRTY FOUR

The Magic of Hawaii

This most isolated and possibly the most beautiful spot on the planet, with no land for over 2,000 miles in any direction, the Hawaiian chain of islands are still untouched by many of the obsessions of modern society, and I believe, no, I know, hold many an essential key to the future of the planet. So much of their teaching is about keeping the memory of that magical part within us alive and well. The part we now call The Unicorn. *152*

THIRTY FIVE

The Hula

I am not Hawaiian, therefore do not consider myself to be accredited as any kind of teacher of Hawaiian ways. I simply share what I have seen and learned with deep love and gratitude. Here is one example of many which at first deny credibility.

More powerful than any martial art there is the Hula. The energetic field created by the pure form of Hula is the one spoken of by mystics such as Rumi.

Some day we will all meet there. *158*

THIRTY SIX

Learn to Heal Yourself!

Connective Tissue: The missing link to your physical healing! The largest system in the human body, connective tissue, also known as fascia or myofascial, has the inherent capability to save your life or, if left untended, to limit both your life quality and duration. Yet it is altogether ignored in medical training . . . in fact, students are told just to tear it out and throw it in the garbage when dissecting corpses as it has no purpose! The largest living system in the body has no purpose? It's like how we're told we have junk DNA! God doesn't make junk, so what is being hidden from us here? The unvarnished truth will astound you and change your understanding of your body for ever! *163*

THIRTY SEVEN

Uncovering the Peace in Any Conflict

If your family conflict seems beyond repair, think again. As the Peace Troubadour, James Twyman teaches, a peacemaker is not one who creates peace in a situation. It is someone who uncovers the peace which already exists beneath the layers of discord and the pain. Using his methodologies peace can be brought to any family, anywhere when they are ready to allow it.   ***169***

THIRTY EIGHT

The Secret of All Secrets!

Now you are ready. Let me now prove, beyond all doubt, what it is that makes The Unicorn so feared by those who control you. If you have not already freed yourself, you will now.   ***173***

Epilogue   ***175***

Role of Honour   ***177***

About the Author   ***180***

Introduction

"The Unicorn is a legendary animal resembling a white horse with a spiralling horn projecting from its forehead. First mentioned by the ancient Greeks it became the most powerful real or imaginary animal throughout the Middle Ages. Commonly described as a symbol of purity and grace, whose magical *third eye* horn had the power to purify poisoned water and to heal all sickness. Only just over a hundred years ago, belief in Unicorns existence was still widespread among historians; physicians; naturalists; theologians; writers; poets and alchemists!" [Google Definition].

What do you feel when you think of a Unicorn? Perhaps childhood thoughts of magic and mystery? For many, a longing that they were once real is common. Now I want you to understand something. The symbolism of this playful magical Unicorn is actually feared by those who think they control you!

This powerful healing and gentle creature is seen chained to the throne of England in royal coats of arms!

Lions, Eagles, Wild Boars, etc. are all present and free on heraldic crests, but The Unicorn alone is chained. Anything that needs to be chained must be deeply feared indeed. That sparkling, magical power of the chained Unicorn is indeed inside of you and the thought that you might remember this, is what most terrifies those who would control the world.

"The Lies That Bind," taught by society, are the chains. Society has deliberately created a "Chicken Coup For The Soul" [pun intended]. When you recognise this and see through these illusions, the power of The Unicorn within you will SWIFTLY return to your awareness and YOUR PROSPERITY IS GUARANTEED!

Prologue

Once, while teaching a workshop in Mexico, my students apologised on behalf of the noisy, all weekend long "Acting Workshop" that was being taught next door. That's when it hit me! We don't need acting classes. We have all become highly skilled actors, role playing automatically in almost every scenario, trying to be whom we are expected to be, depending on the situation, and never quite feeling as though we get it right, hoping we don't get "found out!" How sad and unbelievable is that? We need NON ACTING classes! We have forgotten how to be ourselves and stand in the full glory of our magnificence! The system has us role playing from early childhood and rewards us accordingly.

Most people, still finding it easier to believe the lies we have been fed since childhood, are still scratching around in the confines of the mental chicken coup of misinformation which "appears" to be our reality, rather than challenge the boundaries and finally see them for the illusions they are. What if almost everything we have been taught is a lie? This is not as difficult to comprehend for most of us as it might have been even a few years ago. However, there are so many lies we have been fed that we just don't know where to start to make sense of it all again. The secret is that there is only one lie which has to be uncovered—just one. The rest simply and instantly fall like dominoes once you understand this single truth.

We have been taught that the reality we perceive all around us is the truth, plain and simple, so just deal with it as best we can and we MAY be rewarded for our efforts. That, we have been told, is just common sense. We have also been told that science and technology are the only miracles around and that all glory should be given to its creators. Don't misunderstand me, I truly do admire our scientific genius and thoroughly enjoy the benefits of the miracles of technology each day. The lie that keeps us inside the chicken coup reality is the one that says that only science, technology, governments, schools and churches (all the same thing, all geared to control you) can create miracles and then makes us dependent on their magical capabilities to feed us, shelter us, reward us and protect us.

It is the lie that tells us there is safety and comfort only in scratching around for a living in the chicken coup and that dark and powerful predators, that we should fear, await us, should the walls of that chicken coup ever be breached.

We are taught that magic and miracles are only for fairy tales and for mythical heroes like Merlin, Gandalf and a creature like The Unicorn. That is the ONLY lie you need to see through. What if the reverse were actually true? Merlin, Gandalf and The Unicorn are real examples of YOUR power. What if Miracles and Magic are your birthright and, in fact, are the norm, and that the chicken coup has always been the illusion? What if I can prove it?

Remember this; that those who do not believe in magic will never find it. For those of us who do believe, it's game on! It truly is your choice.

This, then, is a story of how to courageously yet effortlessly embrace the life that you have been waiting for! The stories here will gently liberate you from your fears once and for all. As you read this journey, and identify with the parts which resonate with you, you will understand the chains that have bound The Unicorn within you and will aquire the tools to cut them, effortlessly.

Celebrate the absolute and undisputable proof presented here that "miracles" and "magic" for each and every one of you are only a breath away. The ingredients of this healing recipe to create abundance are not actually an autobiography. They are powerful, yet compassionate and practical words of normal and wondrous human experience, which connect deeply to everyone. These are the tales of our subconscious self-inflicted sabotage, yet our ultimate unavoidable triumph. It is a story that you will instantly recognize as having so many similar parallels to your own.

This journey is different, and while it unfolds in a deliberately woven Celtic Tapestry and mosaic of Past, Present, and Future, it is deeply and deliberately impregnated with true stories of magic and miracles, and will, at some point bring you to the total acceptance that your past and present are inescapably entwined, finally awakening the ancient awareness deep in your heart, and you will see once and for all that you have been creating magic and miracles at every step of your journey through life. You will finally understand the meaning of Free Will and its ramifications as you finally unleash The Unicorn within you.

If you simply allow yourself to connect to the flow of energy in these pages you will receive the tools to understand your past and change your future instantly; no matter what age or gender you may be; no matter what your social or economic situation. The Journey will joyously bounce you from distant past to present, from personal to impersonal, from heart to head and back again. It may well frustrate you a little in odd moments, have you smiling, even laughing in others, yet keeping you open and preventing your focus from becoming too plugged into any one aspect; and from that gentle chaos; allowing the parts that resonate to form in your heart in a sequence that is personal to you and you alone. You will learn to remember the old codes imprinted in your DNA and will regain the means of allowing your entire system to reactivate or reboot itself into the state of peace, happiness and prosperity which truly is, and always was your birthright.

Come to understand how to listen to your heart, which knows that the ONLY THING PREVENTING YOUR PROSPERITY IN ALL THINGS IS YOUR RESISTANCE, placed there by society, religions, families, and cultures since you were born. They have been called "The Ties That Bind." I would like you to think of them differently from now on, they will be thought of as "The Lies That Bind."

See through these "truths" now forever to be known as "lies" and the world becomes a place of wonder and excitement in every heartbeat as you learn how to trust yourself, and, if necessary, forgive yourself for believing the lie of not being "good enough" or "lucky enough" to have and to hold true success, happiness and peace of mind and heart.

You will simply allow your mind to remember and then live your heart's truth, without fear of ridicule or contradiction. I hope most of you will be spared a lifetime of possible turmoil by this story and will teach your children how to continue to see and believe in their truth no matter how things "appear."

They taught you to "Believe it When you See it." From this moment on you know better, and will understand that now you will "See it When you Believe it!"

May this book help you create the world of wonder that we ALL desire, and let it begin today . . . Why wait?

Enjoy the Journey, Much Love, Hugh

ONE

The "Law of Attraction" Was, on One Level, a Deliberate Deception!

What if the viral global message of the Law of Attraction was at the least a subconscious error of delivery or was at worst a deliberate and successful conscious attempt to manipulate mankind onto yet another path of confusion and self doubt?

There is no judgement attached to my statement, it is simply an observation.

The phrase "The Law Of Attraction" has resonated through the Western world for years now leaving millions of people confused, frustrated, empty and even angry as they reject what they feel is just another moneymaking agenda with no real connection to their personal spiritual or physical prosperity.

I believe that subconsciously at least this was the desired effect of the programme.

Let me draw you a fascinating parallel. For 2,000 years (or so they tell us) Christianity, in particular the Roman version, has DELIBERATELY engrained your conscious and subconscious beliefs to focus on the symbol of the crucifixion, the Son of God tortured for YOUR sins, blood dripping, thorns in head, nails through hands and feet et cetera—all with the overwhelming message of it being your fault!

I remember when this was first explained to me. I wondered if anyone in the room realised that I was only three years old, and as far as I knew had never been to Jerusalem! . . . but, thankfully, I kept that thought to myself.

Millions of people did (and still do) venerate this image and hold it to signify the meaning of Christianity and live a life where pain and suffering are expected and considered penance with the only hope of spiritual salvation being firmly placed in the hands of their priests and hierarchies. This control system links hand in hand with Government, who, using the same premise, hold themselves out as "knowing better" and being our only hope of earthly salvation.

How different would this have been if the true ending of the "story" had been the one delivered to the waiting masses of humanity. How happy would everyone have been if the symbol was of the joy of the resurrection, and the implication of everlasting life . . . an event which is freely taught as the actual ending to the story?

The real message, therefore, has always been carefully hidden in plain sight.

Go back to a time when you were first indoctrinated in this tragedy. Imagine you are around 4 years old. How do you feel inside when you focus on a crucifixion and all of its implications? Now give the same attention to the resurrection and the thought of everlasting life.

Which one sets you up best for your day and indeed your life? Which feeling would you like to strive towards or simply allow in yourself? Which feeling would you wish for in everyone?

The former sets your mind up to be controlled and "directed" towards salvation; the latter allows you to feel that certainty of ultimate salvation through your heart.

So what if the same trick has just been perpetrated again? Here we are in the fullness of a time when humanity is finally moving rapidly towards memories of self awareness and freedom from "The Lies That Bind."

The need for a delaying tactic is paramount for those who are losing control. So, just like Christian dogma, what if "They" decided "let's tell the truth again and, once again, focus the spotlight a little off centre"? . . . And so it possibly began.

The whole Law of Attraction premise is founded on the need to create the correct vibration within yourself first, then, what you seek is attracted to you automatically. I agree with this completely . . . however, the phrase pounded repeatedly into our subconscious and conscious minds is the "Law of Attraction" when in essence it clearly is "The Law of Creation" that is the real secret, and the law of attraction is merely a natural validation of this truth.

The second this makes sense the magic can and will assuredly begin for you.

So, to conclude, if the philosophy we were all bombarded with had been entitled "The Law Of Creation," we would all have been home free by now. Before we can attract the right vibration we have to create it inside of ourselves by consistently imagining how it would feel in your heart, your arms and legs, when your wish comes true. Do this as often as you can daily and you WILL begin to see and feel your dreams come true.

So let's get it right then teach our children globally to remember how to do this for themselves.

Here's to "THE LAW OF CREATION" the lost phrase now rediscovered.

This stark truth also exposes the flaws in the premise of Positive Thinking. While it can work it is still putting the cart before the horse, in many ways. This formula for success has been extremely frustrating for many people through the last few decades. So, again, just shift your understanding a fraction and you have the answer. Before you think it, you have to FEEL it! Once you feel the vibration of the state you wish to achieve, the thought process follows automatically.

Let me end this chapter by incorporating a message of hope for all, but in particular to one specific group of forgotten heroes. The Vietnam Veterans are a stunning and unsung group of true survivors of an epic tragedy. They are a group who have endured a lifetime of mental, emotional and physical pain from the horrors they endured as young men in Vietnam and from being ignored and even shunned by their society ever since for a "crime" that has never been defined. They have found ways to survive, although many lived their lives in isolation and torment. My heart goes out to them. One of the songs which they collectively relate to as an anthem is U2's classic hit "I Still Haven't Found What I'm Looking For."

They know, as do we all, that survival is not enough. They are the World Champions of survival. They have been finding ways for 50 years. They want more. They deserve more. They want to LIVE.

Their continued struggle, in part, is because what they are looking for resides inside them, always has. They have forgotten their childlike perfection (and understandably so). I humbly ask them now to add the tool of "Imagining." Imagine what it would FEEL like to be free of their memories, their negative emotions, and their pain; and how being loved, respected and understood would FEEL in their hearts and their bodies. This is not the same as "longing" for peace to appear inside. That would infer that the peace you seek is somewhere "out there." Underneath all the layers of "pain" that has been created in them lies the potential to create a whole new reality only a dream away through the "Law of Creation."

We must FEEL the feeling we are trying to achieve throughout our whole being then gradually, over time the feeling starts to hang around and we begin to feel what we have been looking for.

I just had a client who spent 15 years in the Black Watch Scottish Regiment and was diagnosed with Post Traumatic Stress Disorder, had suffered 2 stress related heart attacks, and whose life has changed on all levels since steadily enforcing the Law of Creation as outlined above.

To all men and women who have suffered trauma (and sometimes are haunted by their own actions in these arenas of conflict) beyond the imagining of most of us, this is where the answer lies.

I understand completely if many of you reading this are still skeptical of my "over simplification." I humbly ask you to continue to read my story and find how easy it is for YOU to manifest permanent change in your life regardless of your situation today.

This book is where your individual and collective sovereignty will be found and will never be taken again.

Let's face it, for the most part, in some way or another we all resonate with the message of the same song and still haven't found what were looking for by focussing on the phrase "Law of Attraction."
. . . Regardless of your "story," and regardless of what you are trying to create in life, I urge you to focus from this moment forward on the "Law of Creation" and let your life unfold.

Namaste

TWO

The Day The Unicorn Was Born and Then Was Chained

I was born in Glasgow, Scotland, shortly after the end of World War II, in an area known as the Gorbals, a district which has become universally renowned for its unparalleled compassion for others, yet also its unparalleled violence, born of the love and the frustration of an Irish Immigrant community, forced to leave their native land due to a manipulated recession and, on arrival, facing massive suspicion and often open hostilities from the resident Scots.

My mother lived there with her Irish parents, and my Dad, an Englishman and a true officer and a gentleman, like many other young men, was in wartime service in the Royal Navy and was, in fact, thankfully returning home unharmed from the theatre of war as I was getting ready to make an entry into the world.

I was soon to move to another working class area, Govan, where I spent my formative years in school, surrounded by the powerful energy of the Clyde Shipyards, watching the jagged metal skeletons of ships being born as they rose high over the walls and hearing the continual metallic clang of hammers shaping steel and the constant fireworks like display of welders torches night and day.

Govan also became an area similar in folklore to the Gorbals, a fiercely proud, big hearted, hard working, hard drinking community, again a place where despite the amazing open heartedness of the area, a mindless violence ran all too close to the surface, in parallel; a place where the people actually lived close to the poverty line in many cases but were not aware of their "status" and lived within a certain tribal code of conduct.

I was somewhat sheltered from the poor living conditions of the area as my father was now attached to the Royal Navy as a civilian, and consequently we had a wonderful large modern apartment wherein I was raised in love and absolute safety in the Royal Naval Reserve H.Q.

However, outside of the R.N.R., life in Govan for most was hard, the air quality often desperately poor from the Industrial Emissions and the coal fired tenement homes, which frequently produced a fog, aka smog, which was so thick you couldn't see the gas streetlights; all sound was deadened, and within seconds black soot particles appeared around your nostrils, indicative of what you were breathing. Many tenement buildings had only a single toilet on each landing for the use of the three families living there, and the river itself was intensely polluted and rat infested..

I returned some years back and was delighted to breathe the clean air and to see that luxury apartment blocks, riverside walkways, restaurants and gardens had replaced the shipyards (although nostalgically I will always miss them), the water was clear in the river, and the thousands of houses were now all self contained and now heated by gas or electricity, no longer pouring out their coal fired pollution.

While I, in my youth, loved Govan and its folk, and still do, there were many times when, like all children, I would vividly imagine and daydream of other lands, which I had only glimpsed in the fantasy created in the local cinema.

My dreams were of America, a country larger than life, the land of Cowboys and Indians, Coloured Televisions, Rock and Roll, Cadillacs, Surfers, California girls, and Endless Sunshine; Canada with its Rocky Mountains, Grizzly Bears, Wolves, Mounties, Blizzards and sense of freedom; South America with Mexico's beaches and Argentina's magical names like Buenos Aires, home of passion and soccer; Hawaii as the ultimate dreamland with its warm waters, hula, dolphins, whales, and sense of peace, all beckoned to me as I sensed a much bigger world outside the, for the most part, very happy confines of my early childhood world. I would frequently imagine how it would feel to actually be in these places, feel the sun and wind, hear the music, swim in the warm waters, drive the convertible, meet the girls etc.

Unknowingly, on a conscious level at least, I see now that I was beginning to trigger and eventually manifest the Law of Creation, and it was certain that I would indeed be in all of these places and more as my life unfolded.

Many times now, on my journey through life, I have remembered my childhood daydreams and pinched myself, wondering if I was dreaming and scared I might wake up, or was I actually living my dream. This sense of wonder, gratitude and humility I felt in the phrase "I'm just a boy from Glasgow" has never diminished and still fills my heart, allowing me to see the world through the eyes of a wee boy from Govan to this day.

Little did I know that my chosen path of Physiotherapy (albeit decided on the flip of a coin!) and my yearning to learn more, would lead me to live my childhood dreams and so much more.

The pivotal moment in my life occurred with a truly massive, tragic and life changing realisation when I was only 10 years old.

I was daydreaming as I walked to school one spring like morning. It suddenly hit me so clearly and "out of nowhere" that . . . I could do anything Jesus did!!! . . . and so could anyone else!! . . . I was no better or worse than anyone, we all have the same "Jesus like" potential! In an instant, it all made totally perfect and undeniable sense!

The thought that Jesus was "God Made Man" not "God dressed up as Man" ran through my mind.

In that instant, I felt the total realisation that Jesus came to show us what we are all capable of . . . "If you only had but a grain of faith you could move mountains" echoed in my head. "What would happen if I had a shovel full?" I mused. Miracles would actually be simple indeed! . . . What if . . . what if indeed?

Ah, I was beginning to actually feel what it might feel like if true and, therefore, by the Law Of Creation, was beginning to subconsciously create my future was I not? That, if true, would appear then to be the life of a world traveller, witnessing and performing miracles in every destination.

How crazy was that? To an adult, ridiculous and pure fantasy, but to a child's heart, anything is possible.

Don't worry, the proof is coming as you read through this book, as you read the tales of travel and the apparent "miracles" uncovered and performed, and you will realise and remember, this isn't just a story about me, it's a story of proof as to what is waiting to be reawakened in you.

Sadly, it was on that day as a ten year old boy that I then made the single most important and devastating decision of my life, although I was not aware of it at that time.

Being raised as a devout Roman Catholic in a large parish with 72 altar boys, I had worked my way up to the envied position of Head Altar Boy, with all of its mafioso like power over the other 71 aspiring Dons and all of the financial fringe benefits of gifts from appreciative families when ceremonies of Marriages, Christenings and Funerals were impeccably presented. There were high hopes from within my family that, as the eldest son, I would enter the priesthood. I could scarcely discuss my revelation with my peers or my family.

I would most definitely have suffered retribution at the very least or even intervention by the clergy at worst. So, I pushed the notion deep into the recesses of my mind and heart, and, stepping back into my brain, I carefully weighed up my options, then I consciously determined NEVER to consider this heresy again, and focussed on my clear imperfections and fallibility as demanded by the church and society, centred myself on getting to school on time, yet with a faint but definite knowing that life would never quite be the same for me no matter how desperately I tried to conform to "The Lies That Bind" and live with the ramifications of my new Law Of Creation.

I reiterate that I now see that this decision, made while meandering to school, created the template for my entire life for the next 50 years with a stunning and often devastating consistency as I subconsciously supported and repeatedly manifested scenarios to reinforce my decision to deny the truth. Within a few short breath taking moments my inner Unicorn had been awakened and unleashed joyously into my reality and within a few more moments I had betrayed it and returned it to its chained and dark posture so deep within the recesses of my heart.

I write this story so that you may remember this still point of your youth, when your decision to deny your perfection was made, and now allow yourself to reverse it, or if you are still a child that you will never feel forced into making such an apparently simple choice for yourself.

Nothing I shall relate is in any way meant to elicit your praise, your sympathy or your judgement, or to demonstrate a victim mentality . . . far from it, it is an awakening as to how the universe aligned to support my decision to ignore my truth and live in "The Lies That Bind." It has done the same for you. There could be no other way.

I repeat that for many readers, this is the time to put the book down, find a quiet space, and reflect on when and where was the defining moment in your childhood when you made the decision to ignore what you knew to be true (to try to fit into the world around you) and now take time to prepare yourself to realise as you absorb this book, how devastating that decision has ultimately proven for you until today.

THREE

Mother/Child Connection . . . Uncovering the Miracle

Let's get back to basics. There is so much evidence of our Merlin like powers all around us that we don't give it a second thought (too busy scratching away in the chicken coup that we believe we live in). We find it hard to believe anything that is outside of that box. That, on some levels has always been a problem for humans who are not switched on, so to speak. Even the Native Americans are reported as wondering why there were strange waves lapping on their shores as Columbus's ships sailed down their coast. They had never seen a craft that large before, therefore, they simply couldn't see the Pinta, Nina or Santa Maria! Eventually they could see them clearly but it took time, even though the evidence was right in front of their eyes. I will present you now with proof of your "miraculous" creating capabilities in the following examples.

In all of my International travels, at some point I ask groups of Mothers if they are telepathic with their children? Their response is ALWAYS the same as they laugh, gently reprimanding me for not seeing that my question is a totally absurd and crazy concept. I wait till the laughter has subsided then ask if I can put it another way. They always agree, and I then continue by asking if they ever know what their children are thinking or feeling?

This question is again met with laughter, only this time they are in agreement with me.

"But of course, all the time" they laughingly respond. "Even as adults my children sometimes get angry when they know I can still tell what they are thinking!" as they nod in agreement with one another.

I continue by asking them what do they call this ability? Almost instantly the response is again dismissive as they define it simply as a mother's intuition. I wait till their laughter subsides yet again, then I quietly ask them if they can give me a scientific name for the ability to know what another human being needs or is feeling? There is always a long thoughtful silence following that question, and gradually, almost in mild confusion they say "Telepathy?" followed by nervous laughter as they begin to understand the natural gift they have all been given but never fully realised or developed. Unknowingly they have just begun to identify The Unicorn within them, after a lifetime of denial.

The following incredible true stories are examples of the miracle of the Mother/Child connection which prove its existence and beg us to investigate it further and help mothers everywhere to fully allow it to blossom into a tool which not only strengthens the bond with their children, but can be the catalyst for the cures of many physical ailments!

The locations are accurate (so you can begin to get the sense that my childhood created visions of travel were indeed unfolding) but the names of the mothers and children have been changed for their privacy. . . .

"The Door Is Opening Mama"

The setting: in beautiful and sultry Puerto Vallarta, Mexico. The place: a Medical Centre for young children. I had worked with many children before, most of them labelled as Autistic in various levels, but honestly wanted to do so in a fully recognised medical facility setting. Thanks to the vision and compassionate leadership in the facility I was enthusiastically given the opportunity; so, here I was somewhat excitedly setting up a portable massage table in a "waiting room/play room" area containing seven or eight young children all displaying different levels of repetitive or hyper activity.

One of the children present in the room was a very bright looking little boy, around 7 years old, and he caught my attention as he bounced constantly on a large inflatable ball. I was about to ask the head behavioural therapist, Kim (herself an amazingly gifted and loving young woman) if she could bring the boy over to the massage table.

Before I could do so, he looked at me briefly then turned his head away from me, holding his arm out between us with his hand up in the "stop" pose, clearly letting me know he understood every word I had said and was not interested!

This did not startle me as I have had multiple verbal and non verbal interactions with these children over the years, some of which can only be explained as telepathic in nature, and, while I don't claim to understand it, I have absolutely no doubt it is a common denominator with many children today.

Next I heard myself saying to Kim "Bring his mother in here!" and, a few seconds later, the somewhat bewildered young mother was standing beside me asking how she could help. I asked her if she would lie on the table while I sat on a chair at the end of it and gently released any muscle restrictions in her neck to help her relax so that her son could see she was resting!

Her first reaction was "No, not me . . . it is my son who needs help!" However, as I gently persisted, she finally agreed and positioned herself as I had requested.

Kim agreed to document anything that happened over the following 20 minutes or so. We were totally unprepared for what followed.

As I gently had my hands holding the mother's neck and head as she rested, she quickly relaxed deeply and was smiling softly. At around the third minute we observed that her son had stopped bouncing on the ball and was watching us intently. He stayed in this focus for a few minutes, then stood up and slowly walked over to stand quietly beside his mother, about half way down the table. Next he very carefully bent her knees before putting a pillow underneath them to support her! Again he simply stood by her side exhibiting complete calmness throughout. Then he walked away only to return with a lightweight cotton blanket and he covered his mother so gently with it, adjusting it from her shoulders to her feet. We were now about 12 minutes into the session and the very calm child was now standing beside his mother's shoulder. He then slowly leaned forward and whispered in his mother's ear "The door is opening Mama!" Kim burst into tears on hearing this and struggled to keep her composure.

The mother was still relaxed and smiling. I gradually took my hands away from her, and we quietly waited for a minute or so before she opened her eyes. She sat up and thanked me profusely, then hugged her son for a long and tender moment before they left the room hand in hand. As they reached the door he suddenly let go of her hand, turned and walked purposefully back to me; looked me in the eye, shook my hand and said "Gracias Senor" before returning to his mother and out of my life.

This had all happened in an exceedingly noisy environment amongst the other children and was a huge factor in my recognition of the stunningly powerful mother/child connection. AS the mother became calm and relaxed, so did the child.

"The Baby Sitter was Amazed!"
Edinburgh, Scotland

Just 2 days after teaching my protocol Kinetic Chain Release (KCR) at Napier University I received an excited email from one of my students. She stated that, to her, the workshop had been phenomenal and that she had "never felt so pain free." She had also taught her 8 year old son the grounding technique she had learned and apparently he was going around teaching everyone how to get rid of the "bad stuff!"

However, what had actually stunned her was the obvious change in her 2 year old son.

For the most part, according to the mother, the boy is non verbal, throws frequent tantrums and does not socialise well with other kids. In the 2 days since Mum came back from the workshop he has been very talkative, saying "thank you" for things done for him, has appeared to be very content and has had NO tantrums whatsoever! Mum says the Babysitter is amazed at the changes!

Remember that the child had not received KCR, only the mother. What a wonderful and true story! This has impacted her so profoundly that, next year she intends to do her Honours Thesis at Napier University on KCR and the Mother/Child Connection.

There is no need to elaborate on KCR at this time as the focus of this story is on the Mother/ Child Connection, not a protocol.

"The Little Drummer Boy"
San Francisco Area, California

Terri Ann had heard through the grapevine that I was coming to within seventy miles of her home and brought her non verbal, autistically labelled, 3 year old son Brett to see me.

Brett appeared as a particularly happy child, an alert, quite tiny little boy, with stunningly piercing and intelligent brown eyes.

As soon as they entered the room I felt Brett connect to me energetically/telepathically and knew immediately that he simply had no reason to talk verbally, he was telepathic, knew that everyone else also has that potential, and could not understand why we weren't using it!

Terri Ann is a delightful, loving single mother who is totally dedicated to her son and was determined that Brett would receive the best care she could provide. However, underneath her vibrant and intelligent exterior I could sense her exhaustion, frustration and fear that she wouldn't succeed. She told me she had strong mothers intuition and often knew what Brett wanted or was thinking without him even being in the same room as her.

Brett busied himself with some toys that Terri Ann had brought, although I still strongly felt his energetic connection to me getting even stronger. So, I went with it and opened my mind to the connection. I told him non-verbally, in my thoughts, that I could see that he was fine and that his mother was clearly the one who was stressed and needed my help. I could feel him being in excited agreement.

I then let him know that I understood that verbalising his thoughts was a ridiculously unnecessary suggestion to him but that to help his mom it would be really cool if he could try to communicate with her more in this manner. Once again I felt the surge of energy that I took to signify his agreement!

The outcome was that Terri Ann agreed to a session with me and she later left feeling revitalised and happy. I told her that I felt that Brett and I had communicated and had come to an agreement and just to go home and let me know how things turned out.

A few weeks passed before I heard from Terri Ann again. Then I received a long email excitedly updating me on their progress. In essence, she said that when she took Brett home that evening he sat on the floor and began drumming rhythmically for hours, then settled down and slept well. The following day he said three new words to her and since our session had now added 120 words to his vocabulary and was increasing them daily. She said his periodic tantrums had also diminished considerably and were almost non-existent!

She was still able to connect with Brett telepathically as before, however, his ability to communicate verbally made life so much easier, especially when around others.

Sometimes it's the child helping the mother. Again in Mexico, we were working on a young mother, as before, and her severely autistic labelled daughter, aged around six, had also stopped her activity to observe, then had come over to us, taken Angie by the hand and led her out of the room!

The second I was finished, the little one appeared in the doorway again and brought Angie back in to sit beside me. Then she waited calmly for her mother to sit up, the mother thanked me and they left together quite peacefully. It was then Angie told me what had happened. When the daughter had led her (Angie) into the hallway, she had made them both sit in waiting room chairs. The little one sat staring at the wall without blinking, behind which lay her mother in treatment with me. Angie said that the child remained extremely focussed on this spot throughout the time there and started to move her hands as though clearing energy from around her abdomen, then her heart, her throat and then between her eyes. Suddenly she was finished, jumped up, and led Angie back into the room at exactly the moment that I had stopped treatment too. Not a word had been spoken.

Can you admit now that there is a strong possibility of a mother/child connection that we are for the most part ignoring? Can you see how it may be used to help children everywhere if we just took the time to explore it a little further? Will you now, if you haven't already, admit that you have a similar miracle making bond with your mother (even if you are adopted) or with your children and that just recognising it is there is like seeing the Pinta, Nina, and Santa Maria. You don't have to know what to do with it yet, you just have to admit to seeing something outside of the confines of the chicken coup.

I have often been asked what about the father/child connection as there are many men who are single parents in today's world and are doing an admirable job of it. I have not seen the changes occur in the children when I work with these fathers, so I do not feel that the connection is as strong, but I will be delighted to be shown differently in the future. However I have noticed how influential the father's energy may be. For example, one man came to see me to deal with a chronic pain issue, which I duly did, and he left pain free and satisfied. His wife called a few days later to say thanks and how much happier her husband was; but also to say that they owned a large dog which was very aggressive towards other dogs and to strangers when it was being walked each day by her husband. Following his session with me he had walked the dog several times and was amazed how well mannered and calm the dog was!

I am totally convinced that many times the behaviours of children and pets are just a reflection of their parents energy, and their behavioural issues can be addressed by working with the parents/owners.

FOUR

Mother Does Know Best!

There are so many heroines out there who are everyday mothers (often single Mothers) who are raising today's labelled children. In my experience, they are a vast source of untapped knowledge that needs to be heard. They often have to find solutions where the medical society has said there are none. I wish we could organise a conference to hear what they have to say. I know they hold many solutions for children everywhere. This is just one such story.

One evening I happened to be watching television and came across the Larry King Show. He was interviewing Bill Cosby and discussing how Bill had dealt with having Autism in his family. I don't usually watch Larry King, but the topic interested me, so I thought I'd listen for a while. Bill was actually trying to give hope to other parents facing similar difficulties and was saying how various therapies, which his family had persisted with, had made drastic improvements in their children's behaviours and personalities. I remember being delighted for him and his kids, yet feeling a tinge of sadness as I knew that the treatments he spoke of were terribly expensive and therefore far beyond the reach of the average families who are the parents of the vast majority of Autistic Children. I knew that if they were watching this show, all it would do would be to give them greater feelings of guilt than they already were living with. Bill was then asked how they first noticed that there may be something wrong with their child. He said that the first thing they noticed was the onset of a sudden lack of eye contact. Their child would not look them in the eye during any conversation and it was as though he was drifting off somewhere else mentally. This became a cause of concern, which they decided to research and, to their horror, discovered it to be one of the cardinal signs of possible impending autism spectrum behaviour. Despite all of the improvements the Cosby's had accomplished, the lack of eye contact was still evident.

I finished watching the show, switched off the television and resumed my own studies and research on many topics of interest to me. Around an hour later I received a telephone call from California. It was from Molly, a young mother of a brilliant young autistically labelled son, Connor. I had the privilege of working with them both on one of my previous trips to the U.S.A. and she would keep in touch and update me on how things were going for them both. She was telling me how she had been told that Connor would benefit from Oxygen Saturation in a hyperbaric chamber, such as is provided by various centres in America. This was way beyond her financial means, so she had researched these chambers and had actually found a small home unit on eBay! She had installed it in her home and, not only was she giving it daily to Connor, and was delighted with the results, she was also offering it free of charge to other mothers of autistic kids in her area! Truly a phenomenal mother. I enjoyed her update and she told me of how these other mothers would discuss their common issues and, in fact, one of them had been the lack of eye contact! Molly laughed as she went on to tell me how she put their mind at ease by telling them that Connor had the same problem but that she had fixed it!

I was stunned as I had just heard Bill Cosby say that all of their therapists had been unable to solve this issue. I knew that Molly would not have seen this as she does not own a television and refused to have one in their home. Molly continued telling me more of their groups discussions, and I actually had to bring her back to the lack of eye contact part of our conversation, as, to her, it clearly had been no big deal! I asked her just how did she regain the eye contact, and she said it was easy. She said that when Connor's eyes would drift off from her she would start singing to him, and, every time she did this his eyes would slowly but surely refocus on her! She said that in case no one believed her she had the home videos to prove it! She went on to say that Connor was her whole life and that she videotaped everything he did! So, here has been just one inspirational story, born of necessity, of how one mother's faith and determination are achieving the impossible. If every mother of an autistic child tried this, and if even 10% of the kids responded, it would be a dramatic step forward. I am just as certain that there are many other mothers out there who have found solutions, but are unaware of their potential to help others and, therefore, do not share. If you know any parents of these types of children please share this story with them, and then take the time to ask them what innovations they have implemented for their own children.

FIVE

Our Narrow Focus is Our Prison!

Our narrow focus has become our prison. We have been taught to focus and analyse everything in laser like fashion, then, in similar fashion, are encouraged to focus constantly on our apparent imperfections (energy flows where attention goes). Thinking outside of the narrow minded parameters we have been given is seldom, if ever, truly encouraged for most children or for that matter, most adults.

So I came to realise that we all have been simply and deliberately led away from our birthright, which is the path of creativity and happiness. According to the chicken coup mentality, we are born "in sin" and consequently we must live a life of trying to prove our worth and never quite succeeding. We will be given awards and rewards if we believe in the chicken coup, we will be given passing grades for regurgitating what we are told to think instead of learning how to think, and blessings of promises of salvation from our churches for being in service. But we will never achieve the perfection in their eyes that we try so hard to attain. Many of our parents, entrapped by the illusion, then impose the same unachievable standards onto their children, and the trap continues to work with deadly efficiency.

The focus has always been deliberately placed on our shortcomings being weighed and judged by society and most of all by ourselves. Does the name Bill Clinton ring a bell? What was the first thought you had of him when you read that sentence? Proves my point, does it not? It is not my, or anyone's place to judge his moral standards or integrity, yet due to one possibly contrived scenario, hardly in itself a criminal act of any consequence, all of the good work he had done was instantly, permanently, erased and his political career over. Yet later administrations could blatantly admit to totally disgusting corruption and acts of appalling violence, and destruction, yet walked away with complete impunity. Where is the perspective?

We have deliberately been taught to live and judge others and ourselves by these criteria and it is an absolutely alien way to live for a human being. The Hawaiians, for example, had no word in their language for "sin." For almost everything where a child thought they had "failed" the people would simply smile and tell them they had missed the mark. Now what would you do if you were told that you had simply missed the mark? You would simply refocus and try again.

One so called "error of judgement" is often held up forever as the marker of our worth while the thousands of compassionate and often brilliant achievements are negated. Just when will we forgive each other for our perceived imperfections? For the minute you can broaden your focus in any situation you, and those around you are truly free.

To crystallize this I give you a poignant Scottish parable:

The young American stood quietly outside of the whitewashed walls of the small local Inn by the water front and harbour of a quaint Scottish fishing village. He took a moment to feel the wonder of the sunset on the calm ocean and he could hear its quiet lapping on the sandy shoreline just to the left of the harbour wall. It seemed like all the world was for just a moment a vibrant yet calming place to be. Giving silent thanks for this incredible feeling he turned and entered the local establishment with its somewhat timeworn stone floors and solid wooden ceiling beams offering an ancient welcome to his spirit. This was precisely what he had sought. Authentic Scotsmen in an authentic environment. He loved hearing their stories of days gone by and their dreams of days to come, along with their ability to talk of legends and enjoy the comradeship of music, song and laughter.

After a while of enjoying the laughter and the banter, he noticed one particular individual who was not engaging in the joviality and was sitting quietly alone, staring reflectively into the crackling warm fire in the old stone fireplace in a corner. Intrigued and feeling somewhat sorry for the man, the American picked up his whisky glass and sat himself down, introducing himself to the quiet soul in the corner. The American introduced himself by name and extended a hand in friendship while asking for the name of the man by the fire. The hand was not accepted, and he let it fall back to his side and decided to quietly sit with this man and be in silence if that was what he wanted.

Ten minutes passed and they sat together sharing the warmth of the fire in silence. The American was considering quietly leaving when the man suddenly said, "My name is Tam." Seconds later he asked "See This Fireplace?" . . . startled, the American nodded an affirmation. The quiet man continued "I built this myself over 50 years ago. I quarried every stone by hand and levelled them and stacked them perfectly, so well indeed that this fireplace and chimney will stand for 500 years. It took me three years to complete and is second to none" His voiced raised slightly as he continued "But do they call me Tam the Hearth Builder? . . . Nooooooooo," he said somewhat mournfully as he resumed his quiet staring into the fire. The American watched him compassionately; an elderly Scotsman, clearly not valued for his worth; then his attention was drawn to the amazing stonemasonry that was before him in the form of this magnificent and intricately formed fireplace, a source of warmth and safety from the storms for untold generations to come. His thoughts were broken as Tam spoke again "See that harbour oot that windae?" . . . The American could indeed see the sheltering harbour wall with many small fishing boats bobbing gently and safely, colourfully at anchor within its boundaries. Again he nodded. After a moment, Tam continued

"I built that myself. No one would believe me when I said it could be done, so I just did it. It took me over 20 years to complete. I asked for help from no man, and I expected no payment of coin in return. But there it is and what a beauty it is. . . . But do they call me Tam the Harbour Builder? . . . Nooooooooo."

After a few more minutes of reflective silence Tam said quietly

"But, just one drunken night in your youth, shag just one bloody sheep!"

"Now ye know my name my friend."

The message in the parable is clear. We focus or are made to focus on our perceived transgressions at the neglect of our successes and loving actions. If "Energy flows where attention goes" how do you think this has played out in your life? Consider that each time you think you are inadequate that you are giving attention to that perception and, therefore, supplying it with energy to create scenarios which will prove that belief?

The Hawaiians would have laughed at Tam and simply said he sure "missed the mark" with that unfortunate decision; then never mentioned it again and focussed on his extraordinary talents and the unselfish gifts he brought to his society.

The focus on the microcosm of our lives and the lives of others, combined with our inability to forgive ourselves or others, has been realized as one of the single most crushing experiences for the human spirit.

So how can you begin to reverse this perspective?

In Hawaii, they have successfully introduced practical exercise to reverse this tendency to narrow focus in their children in the school system with wonderful results. It is called Hakalau and can be implemented by children and adults anywhere.

The children sit and fix their eyes on a spot straight ahead of them. Then they hold their index fingers about 6 inches in front of each eye. Breathing consciously and quietly they gradually separate their fingers, still holding their visual focus on the spot straight ahead until their fingers are at the edge of their peripheral vision. They practice this daily, and within days, they can move their fingers much further back as their peripheral vision improves rapidly.

As the children now see with expanded vision this immediately manifests in other areas. State examiners have commented on the miracle of how the classrooms in Hawaii have become noticeably calmer and alert at exam times! The kids perform Hakalau before they study and before the exams. The effect is that the apparent insurmountable magnitude of the exams has diminished considerably as the kids expand their focus. Prior to this their narrow focus had made the test begin to seem like an all consuming monster in their path. It (the exam) has now become something much smaller and easier to handle and much more in perspective as they see it from the expanded awareness of Hakalau. The passing percentage of children is rising in Hawaii and, of course the kids can apply Hakalau to any problem they encounter in their lives and in society. This can be applied to any problem in your life with only a little practice.

This is also a powerful exercise for those involved in contact team sports such as Rugby, American Football and Soccer. As these athletes develop their peripheral vision they become much more aware of what is happening around them and can react or anticipate much faster.

So why don't you take some time to expand your awareness each day by performing the "miracle" of Hakalau or by simply making a list of all the good things that are part of you, whether you or society recognises them or not? Now expand your focus to include them every time you think of your capabilities. The magic has begun.

SIX

The Young Guns of Patagonia

Everywhere I travel I am blessed with amazing interactions with today's youth. Many of them are gifted in ways most of us don't truly understand. The good news is that their numbers are rapidly growing all around the world. These adolescents and young adults are the future of our planet although they still need a bit of help from time to time as they make the transition. Here is just one of their stories. A story of a day of "miracles."

It was High Noon in Patagonia when my partner and I walked through the rows of parked vehicles and motorcycles and into the bar. There was a hush as we entered the log cabin building on the edge of the high mountain town. Every seat was taken by young adults ranging in age from around 20 to 35. There were a smattering of small children accompanying some of them. The three young men who owned the facility were also brothers. The eldest stepped forward and welcomed us indicating where a space had been cleared in front of the bar for us to erect my treatment table. The brothers took the table from us and assembled it for me, the legs clicking loudly into place in the surreal silence of the normally loud and vibrant atmosphere of the bar. Then the door was locked so no one would be disturbed.

No introduction was necessary. Everyone there knew why I was there, although I was far from certain as to my purpose, but I trusted all was well. I had been working in the area seeing patients for a few weeks and had visited the bar for an evening meal on several occasions. The ambience and the quality of food and drink made it a welcome ending at the end of often a somewhat exhausting days work. Although the staff barely spoke English and I had no skills in Spanish, we managed to engage in conversations, and they were quite insistent that they would like my help, and asked if I would come to the bar on that specific time and day.

I had arranged to have an interpreter meet us there, and it was good to see her come in almost immediately after us. We then simply said "Buenos Dias" to the group and asked who was first?

There was no immediate response until after around a minute, a tall very striking young woman with thick flowing jet black hair and dressed in biker leathers stepped forward saying almost disdainfully to the men that she would go first if they wouldn't. She told me she had low back and neck issues which I was easily able to identify and eliminate within minutes. Clearly delighted to be pain free and fully mobile again she hugged me joyously and returned to her seat.

"Who's Next?" we asked. A young man in his mid twenties, dressed in a black T shirt and jeans stepped up to me, looking me straight in the eyes at all times. The silence in the room seemed to intensify as we stood face to face for quite some time without speaking. Finally, I asked "How can I help you?" Again the silence in the room seemed to increase for around a few moments till he finally said: "I don't want to be angry any more."

It was then that I truly understood the meaning of the phrase "Deafening Silence" as we silently assessed each other and I realised that what I was feeling was, in fact, the combined and focussed energy of the whole group of these wonderful young men and women. They were supporting each other completely and unconditionally, and it truly felt like an honour for me to experience and be enveloped in it.

"I think I can help you," I said and we had some quite open dialogue, covering many facets of his history, along with some physical interactions as I found and eliminated some old injuries. He appeared much lighter energetically when we were finished and was smiling warmly, his dark brown eyes now sparkling almost mischievously compared to the deep pain that been apparent before.

Still no one spoke although many were smiling as he gave me a bear hug like a brother before returning to his table. For the next 3 and a half hours they came to my table and we dealt with everything that surfaced. So much hidden pain in so many of them being released individually and I sensed at times collectively. We all knew when it was over when we all started laughing and talking almost simultaneously.

We had been able to touch that moment in each of them when they made the decision to deny who they were and to attempt to conform to society as was expected of them. The "healing" of their attitudes then was swift and permanent.

The brothers thanked me profusely and in fact everyone gave us much thanks, hugs and laughter as we left, returning to our hotel still deeply feeling the absolute bliss these young people had brought into our lives.

Patagonia was not done with me yet! A few days later I received a message from another young friend there telling me that the psychic children wanted to meet me! Again I was told where and when. It was in a beautiful retreat resort called Pyramides Andines in San Carlos Bariloche . I never did find out why they wanted to meet and how the word had got around, as most of them had clearly never met before our gathering. We showed up on time and were seated outdoors among the lush natural vegetation, along with an interpreter as over thirty young people gathered in front of me. The youngest was around four years old and the eldest possibly late twenties. Some were dressed conservatively with hair well groomed, others very casually attired and hair long and braided. All of them had bright sparkling eyes, either deep brown or piercingly bright blue, all had good personal hygiene and their energy shone around them as they positioned themselves comfortably. I had no idea what this was about and just decided to let the evening flow.

Several were local professional young business men and women; others came from a delegation of young folk who live in the forests of the surrounding Andes Mountains; some never did divulge their background, several more looked like a-typical teenagers, others just kids. Their collective focus on me felt extremely intense indeed, yet utterly loving and supportive. Many things transpired that evening as we all got to know each other better. As I talked about making the decision that changes your life as you force yourself to accept the chicken coup as your reality, they were in silent yet enthusiastic agreement. These young people had never allowed themselves to fall into that situation and therefore were still in a state of total recognition of their potential. Yet there was again so much anger in some of them at the apparent state of the world around them. We were able to work through and release a massive amount of this together that evening. They began to understand their individual and collective talents and accompanying problems much better also. For example, the young adults from the forest were clearly highly telepathic and at one point their leader said that he felt that words were unnecessary. I understood him and in fact from some perspectives I agree with him, however I just sat in silence and waited for the group's response. One young lad probably in his mid twenties, although he looked much younger, spoke up. He said that words to him were extremely powerful. He said that he was an Octagon (*cage*) Fighter (which completely shocked me as he looked so young and not a man you would ever have thought of as a fighter).

He went on to say how almost every week in his social environment he would be challenged to fight, usually by people fuelled by too much alcohol. He said that it was vital that he found the exact words and tone to give those people the opportunity to walk away with dignity intact as he felt that if he had to prove himself by hurting them that would be failure on his part. His words here received nods of approval from all gathered there, including those from the forest. We talked for over three hours and one of the many, many fascinating things was the young children there. Some were little more than infants, yet they sat on their parents laps throughout the gathering, never becoming restless or distracted. Their eyes remained fixed on each speaker and they never missed a word of what was said for over three hours. Once again, we all suddenly knew when it was over and with many deep hugs and much laughter and gratitude this gathering of such beautiful souls ended.

I never saw them again but my heart sings as I recall the pure love these young ones possess and share so willingly. I am certain that there are millions just like them around the planet who will not deny their truth as most of us did, and who are creating a dimension of peace and abundance on our planet. These young ones are acutely aware of their Inner Unicorn and support each other constantly in its nourishment and growth. Do the words "and a child shall lead them" start to ring true yet with you? Can you see that these young ones, holding their light so confidently and clearly, are the example for us all? Do you understand that the abundance you seek is literally only a creative dream away?

SEVEN

The "Law of Creation" Unfolds, and The Unicorn Remains in Chains and Darkness Within Me

The other side of the coin. My decision to deny my revelation of my (our) potential when I was 10 very quickly took shape in physical manifestations in the world around me. Looking back now I clearly see that it was shortly after this that I suddenly became the target of severe, sustained and prolonged bullying at school for six years, something I felt helpless to avoid, although bewildered as to why it had begun so suddenly. I couldn't fight back as the dockside mentality around bullying was often built on how many brothers, cousins etc. the bully had to back him up, not on how well he could fight. Being an only child at that time.

I had no such family framework to rely on and I also knew if I truly fought back my very life could be endangered by the retribution from older siblings etc. who considered life to be a very cheap commodity at best. So each day became about survival and my true thoughts and reflections were indeed suppressed and ignored as I had intended with the Law Of Creation. Expressing my self spiritually or even intellectually resulted in even greater repercussions of "punishment," even from certain teachers, so I, like millions of others, hid deeper and deeper inside myself, trying desperately to appear to conform. My growing lack of self esteem, the exact opposite truth of our reality, which I had so clearly realised and rejected on that bright spring morning years before, was further cemented and compounded by a shattering event at a Scout camp when I was thirteen. Remember I was now deliberately, and with great sadness, creating an energetic of imperfection (which I believed I was supposed to believe) which would naturally be reinforced the harder I tried to believe it !

I still was recognised as a bright lad and was allowed to attend events usually held for kids a bit older so I was excited and grateful to be given the opportunity to attend this particular jamboree. The "shattering" event I refer to was what I was told was my initiation, which of course a boy must forever keep secret, but in effect was my nightmare as I was held facedown by several 16 and 17 year olds and ritually abused. This must have been quite traumatic to my spirit as I totally blocked it from my memory until gradually, clearly and most unwillingly I began to recall it all graphically around 20 years ago.

[Interestingly though, if I may digress for a moment, there were many moments of real clarity in the somewhat tortuous process of several years of eventual healing. Seeking counselling back then felt shameful, terrifying and humiliating, yet ultimately necessary, or I wouldn't have survived. Meeting so many other men from all walks of life in my "group" who had survived similar outrages in their boyhood was initially uncomfortable yet ultimately a revelation. Their courage was remarkable and the fact that they had survived at all, far less lived outwardly successful lives, was a testament indeed. When we took our breaks, we had to take them at a different time from the female group down the hall as many of them were understandably "distrustful" of men. It hit me so clearly that by this separation we were reinforcing the gender bias. These groups should eventually in the process be merged into one (individual counselling still available as required). We were all simply children whose innocence was brutalised. That was the common factor. Whether we were male or female was never the issue. Our pain was the same. Unity would have been a massive step forward at that point and I hope that someone reading this has the power and courage to implement it where appropriate.]

The episodes of bullying and Initiation had been effective (as I had subconsciously planned) in as much as they reinforced my decision that I was FAR from perfect and that the way was indeed one of attrition as I focussed on following the path taught by "The Lies That Bind."

Can any of you reading this now see where your decision to "hide your light" or to deny your possible perfection has manifested similarly, be it subtle or graphic in nature, to my experience(s) and has fulfilled your desire to deny yourself ever since? It can be quite a shattering yet empowering realisation when it finally hits you.

You did what you did simply to survive and to fit in, a normal response for most, but the price you have paid for this denial may have been more heart rending than any decision to accept the truth would have been, as the Law of Creation manifested around you.

This realisation that I and I alone created my life based on my beliefs has made forgiveness of others a simple thing indeed, although forgiving myself for my actions towards others along the way has not been so easy.

EIGHT

A Telepathic and Clairvoyant Child, and Another, and Yet Another . . .

As I finally began to be aware of my inner Unicorn again . . . the magic began to unfold. . . .

I was blessed to meet Sophie in Calgary, Western Canada, when she was about 8 years old. She was yet another beautiful child I had been privileged to meet who had been labelled as Autistic and non verbal. I knew as soon as we met that she was telepathic and clearly felt her "scanning "me as seems to be the norm for these kids. Her mother was doing her best as a single Mom to raise her daughter as best she could (and doing a splendid job I might add!) and they lived together in a small apartment over some local shops. Mom had known that Sophie was telepathic since shortly after her birth and they communicated back and forth constantly. However she was understandably extremely guarded about sharing this awareness with others for fear of ridicule or worse.

The mother was also quite shocked to realize that, by the fact that she could understand Sophie non verbally, she herself was considered telepathic!

As our first meeting was actually at a group community meeting I settled into the agenda and was sitting sideways on to Sophie who was sitting with her back to me about 10 metres away, playing with her "toys." Several times in the following hour I felt Sophie's energy tuning in to mine, getting stronger each time. Finally I turned my head to look at her, and almost immediately she turned almost fully around to engage me in eye contact!

I smiled at her and turned back to my group, then decided to play a game just to see for myself if it was all coincidental. Totally distracted now from what was being discussed around me I waited a few minutes then periodically turned to look at Sophie. Every time she immediately had the same response, turning around to hold eye contact. I didn't know what exactly was transpiring between us but I felt very focussed and peaceful although somehow Sophie's energy was calming my mind and spirit. We held each other's gaze silently for what was only a few seconds, but felt much longer.

I felt remarkably peaceful for the next day or so and I firmly attribute that to Sophie's energetic gift.

Now, in retrospect I realise that I was simply allowing myself to sense, or see, the true light within her and allowing her to access mine.

Interestingly enough, some time later, the local shop below their apartment was burglarised during the night and the following morning the police came up to Sophie and her Mother's apartment to see if they had seen or heard anything unusual. Her mother said that Sophie had slept peacefully beside her all night and they had not heard anything unusual. While mother was giving her statement to the police Sophie was doodling on paper at the kitchen table, or so it seemed until she walked over to the officers and handed them the paper on which she had drawn a remarkably accurate portrait of three individuals including what they were wearing!

I never did hear how all of that ended as I left for pastures new and so did Sophie and her mother but I'm sure she is still astounding everyone she meets and I hope that by now she has been able to connect physically or telepathically with other similarly gifted children or adults.

I will never forget the peace I felt when Sophie focussed her energy on me, even with her back turned to me. What a gift these kids bring to us all, the "miracle" of inner peace, if only we were open to accepting it from them.

On another occasion I was asked to go to St. Louis, Missouri to see some "autistic" kids and what a blessing they proved to be! There was Sid, a very tall seventeen year old, non verbal youth, diagnosed as severely autistic and mentally retarded. I went in to see Sid and he was wearing his mp3 player earphones playing Beatle's music, and also wearing a protective helmet; pacing rapidly up and down the room, occasionally going to stand on a mini trampoline and bouncing on it for short periods.

I just sat quietly and observed as Sid seemed to be walking a little closer to me each time he moved back and forth in the room. I simply focussed on "seeing" or "sensing" the light in him that is in us all and waited, with no agenda to see what, if anything would happen. He suddenly stopped, walked right up to me and put his face inches from mine, staring into my eyes for almost a minute. Again I felt the deep and timeless sense of peace that I had felt when Sophie connected! Then Sid walked over to his wonderfully patient, compassionate and intellectually gifted therapist and began to hit what seemed like random letters on the word board which he could sometimes use for basic communication. He would hit only two or three letters at a time, then go back to bounce on the trampoline, then repeat the process many times. We were all stunned as the letters began to spell words until a sentence was formed.

Sid had typed "Can we move this meeting to a more ambient setting!" And this was from a lad labelled as retarded by the school system, who, by the way, would not allow the use of the word board in school, stating that it wasn't a scientifically proven tool!!

What a waste of a gifted child. I believe that simply recognising him heart to heart as I did was all he and the other children ever needed. I later heard that Sid asked about me often and further than that his tantrums of frustration were almost non-existent and he could even travel by airline to see relatives, a feat which would have been impossible before.

I believe this what we all need. Just to be seen for who we truly are, accept the wonderful vibration of peace and love that they offer us every time they meet us, or maybe every time they think of us, and the magic begins immediately. Can you now see the need to simply drop the labels that society has given us and that you have given yourself and take a moment to recognise the wondrous potential in yourself and in us all?

When you look at others you interact with or pass by each day can you allow yourself to see that light in them, even though they have forgotten it themselves?

Can you focus gently deep inside yourself, breathing quietly into your heart for just a few minutes each day, knowing that the same energy/light rests hidden within you? It can be done in solitude, or while driving to work, or returning, or on awakening each day.

Just that knowing that there is such a place of dreams within you is enough for now.

[Footnote: My father recently passed away after five devastating years of Alzheimer's, a cursed affliction which has truly has been named "The Long Goodbye."

At the times when it was at its height and my father, a highly intelligent man, had no cognition of who we were or where he was, or what his watch was but could only mutter incoherently, I would sometimes sit and allow myself to see the light hidden so deep within him. Amazingly at times we definitely connected. He would suddenly lock eyes with me and I would briefly feel the same peace of connection that I had experienced with Sophie and Sid. Therefore the same principles should apply to all of our interactions daily.]

However we can't always help when others with control cannot see the energy/light in themselves or others.

While in St. Louis I was taken to see "Danny." It was a dark, winter's windy evening and the bare branches of trees waved wildly across the Illuminated sign "Children's Asylum" as I pulled into the dimly lit driveway. After passing through several layers of security I was allowed into Danny's room.

I sat there utterly stunned and horrified at what I was seeing and what I was feeling.

Danny was labelled as severely autistic and non verbal, and had recently become much more aggressive at home and had also taken to banging his head repeatedly and forcefully off of the walls. Medication had not minimised these behaviours so he was institutionalised for his own safety.

So here now in front of me was Danny in a bare cinder block walled room. He was spread-eagled on top of the bed and his wrists and ankles spread and shackled to the four corners of the bed frame.

This is not a criticism of the institution or of the staff who appeared to be very caring indeed as I chatted with them later. They were simply restraining Danny in the only way they found that worked.

My heart went out to Danny, lying there writhing and crying aloud. I tried to connect to his inner "light" and was met by what I can only describe as a white wall of intense pain, so powerful that I simply couldn't seem to get through it even a fraction. I realise now that Danny was allowing me to see the inner torment he was experiencing. After almost an hour I surrendered and eventually left Danny and the facility. I felt absolutely shattered and in complete despair for this poor child in such torment and restrained in every sense of the word. I never did see Danny again.

Some months later his therapist wrote to me telling me of a story she had come across of another autistic child who suffered just like Danny but somehow had made a full recovery and could now communicate slowly but clearly. He said that his headaches created pain beyond imagination and he found that each time he smacked his head against a wall the pain would diminish for a split second. "And then you put me in restraints and the pain never went away even for a second. It was like having King Kong pounding inside my head day and night," he said.

On reading this I thought of Danny and I felt sick to my stomach. A little cranio sacral therapy could well have eased his symptoms. Surely it should at least have been tried. Medical marijuana in tea. Not tying him down and walking away! We all need to share a tear for Danny and all of the other children facing similar horrors. If we would all try just a little, or maybe a lot, harder to see the light/source in all of these children from, or even before, birth we WILL be able to create a reality where these devastating symptoms and misunderstandings occur.

However, once again I reinforce it has to begin with recognising the part of ourselves that has been betrayed and forgotten deliberately by "The Lies That Bind."

NINE

Clearing the Land . . . Montana U.S.A.

The concept of clearing stuck or negative energy from land would have struck me as a strange and even bizarre concept in my early life. However, as I have come to understand the energetic principles involved it just makes sense. Now I am called intuitively and frequently also by personal request to attend many sites throughout my Intercontinental Travels. Like doubting Thomas, I have learned to always ask my God/Higher Power to give me proof that what I did or do was/is not crazy or ego driven and also in some way was effective. This day the miraculous proof was stunning and immediate and I have the photographs to prove it to myself in case I ever doubt the wonderful reality of the day at the Little Big Horn River in Montana U.S.A.

I awoke with a start. The setting sun was just behind the rolling hills to our left, shadows beginning to lengthen on the lush grasslands and the moon was already above the horizon to the right.

We were driving back to Canada after I had been speaking at a Global Event for Integrative Medicine in Santa Fe, New Mexico and I had been asleep as my partner Jane took her turn at the wheel.

I felt almost mesmerised by the beauty all around us and softly asked "Where are we?"

"Wyoming, honey," she replied. Instantly I thought of the Plains Native Americans who once roamed there; Sioux, Cheyenne and others. I could easily visualise and sense the presence of the incredibly large herds of buffalo here. I could also feel, and "see" or vividly imagine massive herds of wild horses everywhere around us as ancient memories flooded into my awareness. I didn't speak again until we pulled into a hotel for the night in the town of Casper, Wyoming.

That night I slept the most peaceful sleep I had felt in years and awoke incredibly calm, focussed, and totally in love with Casper, Wyoming!! It was such a deep resonating connection, one that I never remembered feeling before although I feel connected to many places.

Jane remarked on my demeanour and asked what the plan was for the day. I heard myself say

"We're going to clear the land at Little Big Horn." I had never said this before in my life, yet somehow I sounded quite matter of fact about it all.

Jane, as usual, was not surprised, it was on our route back home to Alberta and she simply began getting us ready to hit the road again after a quick and much enjoyed breakfast.

To explain, the meandering Little Big Horn River is the site of the Battle between Gen. George Armstrong Custer and his 7th Cavalry of around 240 men and a massive gathering of thousands of Sioux and Cheyenne Plains Indians. The tribes never thought that Gen. Custer would be so foolish as to attack such a large and peaceful gathering, but he did; the warriors protected their women and children; and the Seventh Cavalry were quickly massacred to a man.

 It has been known as Custer's Last Stand historically, yet, in reality it was the Chiefs Sitting Bull and Crazy Horse and their people and their way of life's last stand as, following this tragedy, the U.S. Government relentlessly hunted and exterminated them across hundreds of miles until they, as a once proud nomadic people, connected to the land and nature, were no more, and those remaining alive were put on "reservations" totally dependent on the white man for subsistence.

So I tend to think of the place by the Little Big Horn as "Sitting Bull's Last Stand."

As we drove through Wyoming, north into Montana, I was still acutely conscious of the same energies that I had felt the previous evening and, around noon, on a devilishly hot early June day, we pulled quietly into the half full car park at the site of the Battle of The Little Big Horn.

I had been there once before, some thirty years earlier with my wife and young sons and had felt quite connected to the region. I think I should relate that experience first so you may understand the story of what happened on this, my second visit. Back then, I had followed the trail through the battlefield from the back to the front. [The Visitor Centre is situated near the spot where the Cavalry made their last stand—but the battle actually only culminated there—it began some miles back along the ridge where Major Benteen and his cavalry had attacked the rear of the massive gathering of tepees while Custer and his men raced along the ridge overlooking the camp, hoping to move in a pincer movement and defeat those camped there, so, if you ever go there, it is better to drive back to the beginning and slowly work your way forward to where it all ended.] Benteen was quickly beaten back and retreated up the side of the ridge where the survivors dug pits behind their dead mules/horses and spent a long day or more pinned down, beneath a blistering hot sun, by extremely accurate Sioux sniper fire (although it would appear that there were only 2 or 3 "snipers" there to keep them immobile while the rest gathered up their families and their belongings and moved off after Custer's men had been dealt with).

As my family moved along the trail we found a solitary marker stating "A U.S. Cavalry man fell here." Then we would find two together, then four, then more and more scattered around in increasing numbers until we came back to the spot with many markers, where, surrounded and hugely outnumbered, the remaining troops formed a circle and were soon overcome. However, as the chain of command finally dissolved in the madness of battle, a small group of men broke out from the circle and ran blindly down into a nearby small canyon, where they were quickly found and killed, apparently buried together in an unmarked grave (although why the military precisely marked the spots where the other men fell, and reburied them in the military cemetery,and not these poor terrified souls I can only speculate)

It was at the unmarked grave of these men that I decided to start, on my return 30 years later.

I asked God/Spirit to help me do the right thing as we steadily walked down the slope on a narrow well worn path to where those "unmarked" men lie. I think I am fairly confident as to the location of this resting place and we were able to easily get within 20 metres of it (although I do feel the bodies have now been moved).

It was as we were getting close to this spot that the first of many "strange" things happened.

It was a hot summers day with barely a breath of air (as it had been on the day of the conflict) and it seemed just a little strange that we were the only ones on that path, yet there were many visitors up above us on the hill at the fenced site of the last stand. Then we became aware of a new and increasing continuous sound "Thock . . . Thock . . . Thock." Looking to my right I saw a military helicopter moving, it appeared, almost in slow motion, towards us from the direction of the Little Big Horn river. It was an older helicopter and it seemed to move so slowly and actually stopped, hovering, no more than 20 metres in the air, right in front of us. We could clearly see the faces of the flight crew as they regarded us for a few seconds then slowly moved off over the last stand markers and disappeared over the top of the hill to cross the prairie like grasslands beyond.

Several things registered briefly in my mind at that time but I put them away to hold my focus on my purpose for being there. Things like . . . there was no downdraught from the chopper . . . the 7th Cavalry are now an airborne unit . . . no one at the top of the hill seemed to notice as the helicopter flew directly over them, much closer than it had been to us!

I focussed on the souls of those originally buried here in this sacred spot and began my ritual. In essence it has become a combination of "protocols" with the underlying emotions of Understanding, Compassion, Love and Forgiveness given and received between myself, the land and those whose lives ended there, until I feel the deep and often heavy energy of the area change, then I move on. Within a few minutes I felt a distinct lightening of the energy around us and knew that I was finished at that spot. With a sigh I turned to walk back up the path and was stopped by a large snake which slowly moved across the path not a meter in front of us. I was still in the *energetics* of the moment and we felt no threat from its presence, rather we felt blessed to have seen it and took it as a good sign that all was well.

I was then drawn into the military cemetery further up the slope, where the bodies were finally interred, and, after quiet contemplation, I was drawn to one specific "Unknown Soldier" Gravestone and knew this was where I should begin next.

I began by asking the spirit of the soldier there if I could work with and through him. I felt an instant peaceful acceptance of my request and so began my work, asking that any other spirits there which wanted to participate should feel free to join me also. After a few meditative moments I was amazed as not one or two, but what appeared to be thousands of spirits joined us! There were US Cavalry; Native Americans; Buffalo; Wild Horses and Eagles stretching around my mind's eye as far as I could see in every direction and then I very clearly felt that what had happened here was an agreement made by many souls to play out the necessary drama between the two cultures in this sacred energetic vortex, beside the Little Big Horn river in Montana!

I heard the words of Chief Black Elk who witnessed the last group of soldiers fleeing down into the gully where they met their end. He said:

"Their arms were moving very fast, like they were running, yet they were walking."

Clearly no one was going to escape their destiny that day! I felt that this necessary defining moment in time was unavoidable and I also strangely felt that many souls had made a pre-life agreement to participate in this monumental event. I would have laughed aloud at anyone who talked this way to me before, but the feeling of "knowing" was so strong that I could not denounce it in any way. I did not understand it, I simply knew it to be true.

As I worked, the energy seemed to clear around me, until I thanked all those assembled there for the role they had played in the past and here today in the present, and, first taking a few deep stabilising breaths, I opened my eyes. I was stunned at how much brighter and clearer everything looked all around. It was as though a warm glow pervaded everything and I felt such a deep peace as we quietly returned to my truck and drove back along the ridge to pay my respects to the area where Major Benteen's troops had been pinned down and where Gen. Custer had last been seen alive.

Everything looked and felt so different. The energy from the land itself had a sparkling, delightful texture to it, revealing itself as the vortex it always had been.

Feeling the same peacefulness I had felt since entering Wyoming the previous day, we got back in my truck and prepared to leave. I thanked God/Spirit for giving me such an uplifting experience and then I asked for a sign that what I did was not a figment of my ego or of my imagination. I asked that it be a sign so clear that I could not mistake it or misinterpret it. I also said that if there was no sign given, that I was ok with that as I was simply happy to feel such peace.

Less than two minutes into our journey back along the ridge we rounded a corner in the trail and I was given the sign I had requested! I could hardly believe my eyes as I pulled the truck over to the side and stopped, asking my partner if she could grab our camera, which she just happened to have at hand.

Racing up from the expansive gently sloping prairie to our right, cutting off my truck from progressing, was a very young wild horse, a dark brown yearling with a white blaze on his forehead; followed by a huge black stallion, muscles rippling and mane flowing as he seemed to almost glide behind the colt. Then, behind them, came a herd of around fifty wild horses, mares and colts, young stallions, Black, White, Light Brown, Dark Brown, Grey, and Pinto, following the young one as they raced straight at us!

Suddenly, another pick-up truck sped by us from behind and slowed down a hundred yards ahead of me, probably as equally stunned as we were to see these magnificent animals at such close range.

Immediately the herd slowed to a walk and the Black Stallion broke away to attack the truck! It seemed enormous and incredibly powerful as it raced towards the truck and reared up on its hind legs threateningly. The truck driver threw his vehicle into gear and accelerated wildly off in a cloud of dust, no doubt going to report to the Park Rangers that he had just been chased off by a wild stallion! Of course the chances of the rangers believing him would be slim to none!

As the stallion turned back to join the herd, they began to form a single line and, still following the young colt, raced past my truck, each one leaping and bucking with joy as they passed; then after passing us, still at a full gallop, they formed up into full herd formation again, and then they veered away, thundering off on to the prairie again until they disappeared into the horizon!

We sat there for quite a while, totally lost in the beauty and magnificence of what had just happened, then, almost reluctantly, slowly completed our journey through the battlefield and pointed our truck north to Alberta and our home in Calgary. The intense feelings of peace and such bright energy quickly faded as the miles rolled away, but the memory and miracle of it all is easily accessed any time I close my eyes and allow myself to remember.

TEN

Manifesting a Life of Denial and Separation

Now we slip back in time to the formative years and consider how I was manifesting a life of denial and separation as I had requested via the Law of Creation. Feel the different energetic between this chapter and the last.

As my early teen years developed the self fulfilling desire I had been projecting for myself, my sense of separation from others and my imperfection only deepened and was continually reinforced.

I remember how some remnants of belief that just maybe we were all perfect still clung on just below the surface, so I had to prove that this could not be the case at every opportunity.

One example was in Mathematics. I had developed the ability to solve every math problem put in front of me (age appropriate) but I had no idea how I had come up with the answers!

[My inner Unicorn knew but was kept in submission and silence.]

One day, after an exam, at around 13 years of age, I was hauled out in front of the class by the teacher, a sadistic hulking bully of a man who delighted in terrifying and physically hurting children as often as the opportunities presented themselves. He produced a paper I had submitted with every answer correct although I had no methodology in place. This was long before Blackberry's and iPhones so I had no means of eliciting outside help for my answers.

The towering teacher demanded to know who I had copied the answers from. If he had just looked around the class seating arrangements he would have seen that no one within any reasonable distance of me had got the answers correct in the test therefore copying would have been a pretty futile activity for me. Knowing that this information would simply humiliate him and enrage him I decided to keep quiet on this and simply re-affirmed that I had not cheated. This actually seemed to be the answer he was hoping for! He was now able to bring out his legendary leather strap, a long thick, almost rigid instrument of legal corporal punishment, and after a few practice swings informed me that I would be punished until I told him how I had cheated. I had to extend my arms, one hand below the other, palms up as he whipped the strap down onto them, changing hands each time. I, of course, had nothing to say as there was no story I could make up even if I wanted to.

After about 12 strokes my wrists were both swelling badly and the fire in my hands was intense indeed. Then a small quiet awareness in my mind clearly let me know that this man was not going to stop until I cried! That had been his purpose all along! Almost reluctantly and in somewhat humiliation I allowed the fiercely held back tears to roll down my cheeks, and after keeping me standing there quietly crying for a minute or so, he dismissed me disdainfully with the warning that the punishment I had just received would be mild compared to what would await me if I ever "cheated" again. My lesson had been learned yet again. Dare to consider that you may be perfect and enjoy your miracles and you'd soon find out different. I buried my truth even deeper inside and never again did I submit correct answers for mathematics. This was cemented deeper by a further confrontation with a bully with a number of elder brothers renowned for their violence, who made it clear that if I finished higher in grades than him I would be beaten and stabbed on my way home from school! At this point I genuinely stopped connecting with the learning process almost completely and could see no way forward other than survival until my schooldays were at an end.

The same teacher would sneer at me each time he handed me back my "failed" submissions from that day forward but while I never faced his physical abuse again, my inner rage at myself for not being who I was and continually flying under the radar, began to grow and manifest in other ways.

[Footnote: one day around 10 years later I saw this teacher in the crowd at a football (soccer) game in Glasgow. In an instant I had exploded with rage and it took all of my friends to hold me back as I tried to get at him. I thank them for this as I have no doubt that I, no longer a child, would have caused him grievous bodily harm should I have been able to reach him.

Yet still I persisted in my decision of that 10 year old boy to suppress who I genuinely was and try to fit in. How many of you can empathise with this and, if so, can you realise that you actually created it through your belief system and the Law of Creation?]

ELEVEN

Happy "Soul Soup" Stories

A sprinkling of miracles! Church bells were ringing. Masses were being offered. Street parties were erupting. The following are all touching stories of how miracle status was given so many times, in a short space of time, where it was in actuality quite explainable and, more importantly, teachable. My Unicorn is very much free again here.

I was working in an area in Mexico where poverty was close to the surface for many. The people however, were always clean, tidy and happy folk with a good sense of community and pride. It was such a lovely place to work. First I saw a fourteen year old girl who could only walk on tip toes, her knees rubbing together with every step and was completely unable to run. She had undergone surgery to both knees and the physicians had told her family there was nothing more that could be done for her. Following application of KCR and Connective Tissue Release, just twenty minutes later, she not only walked normally, but had her father in tears as she happily ran up and down the hallway, gaining speed and confidence each time!

Another father brought his beautiful young daughter to see me. She was twelve years old and was wearing full length metal braces on her legs. She had worn them for years to help correct her from turning her feet inwards when walking. The doctors had told her to come back when she was thirteen, when they would cut off her right leg, change the angle to her hip and re-attach the limb with screws and plates!

Then, when she turned fourteen they would do the same to her left leg! Her thirteenth birthday was fast approaching. We got her out of her braces and, on examination, I felt that it had probably been an injury at birth that had created the imbalance, so I worked on her for about an hour, correcting some of her imbalances with KCR then releasing connective tissue restrictions around her hips and pelvis. I could feel vivid changes happening in her alignment as we worked together. When finished I got her to stand up and see how her feet would place themselves on the floor. Not only were both feet almost straight, she slowly walked up and down the room, with no pain or instability! We were all ecstatic, her most of all. Her smile seemed to light up the world! After teaching her a few easy stretches to sustain the changes, we were on our way back down the coast to the community where we were staying.

We heard sometime later that, after I had left, the word of their "cure" had quickly spread around the community, church bells were ringing, masses being said and joyful street parties exploding spontaneously into life all around in celebration of the "miracles."

On another day we had driven down to the city of Colima, a beautiful drive through lush jungles where, we were told, condors, jaguars and anacondas abound. The only part that was not so enjoyable was when, on rounding a curve on the narrow road, our path was blocked by a group of ten, very serious looking men armed with enormous automatic rifles, bandoliers of ammunition across their chests!

I do not speak Spanish so sat quietly as our passports were requested and our driver conversed with their leader for over five minutes. Suddenly the mood changed as they both began to laugh and jest with each other before the men stepped aside, smiling and waving cheerfully to us as they let us continue on our way. Apparently they were drug enforcement police officers who try to stem the massive flow of drugs through these areas and whose lives are often endangered. As their leader talked with our driver it turned out that she had dated his kid brother in high school and he actually remembered her fondly once she identified herself! Very relieved we quickly drove on through the jungle.

We spent a few days treating patients in Colima and before leaving we were asked to go visit an elderly lady and her family. She was a lovely matriarch, around ninety years young surrounded by a loving family of children, grandchildren and great-grandchildren. She was in

....g frame to use only to help her and her family to transfer her to the toilet seat or into her bed.

I simply decided to see the light/energy inside her the same way I did with non verbal kids. I sat beside her and placed one arm around her with my hand between her shoulder blades and we both seemed to meditate quietly for a few minutes. Yet again, that familiar peaceful feeling came up inside me and stayed there even after we had broken contact. When it was clear that she and I had concluded our interaction, everyone began talking again and family banter and laughter filled the house. Suddenly someone yelled "Look!" and pointed at their great-grandmother. Everyone stopped in stunned silence as they watched her walking across the room using her walking frame to get into the toilet! She had not walked unassisted for some years. She was smiling, almost mischievously, as she glided across the large room and closed the washroom door behind her. Just recognising the magical light within another human being was yet again proven to be all that was required. You know, I think that the greeting used in the movie "Avatar" which was "I See You" may have much more relevance than it has been given (and I suspect was quite deliberately put into the script!).

Later, in a fairly large city in Western Mexico we had been invited to visit the children in a large Kindergarten, to see how my work may benefit them. I was hoping to do a quick study and see just how many 5 year olds were exhibiting the physical signs of imbalance caused by an apparent shortening of one leg compared to the other. The children had other plans for me that day.

In a large room we found there were well over 100 children, supervised perfectly by only 5 young adults. We were struck by how well behaved and happy everyone was, not one child creating a ruckus and everything just seemed to flow beautifully as they played games and sang songs together. I was introduced to them as Dr. Gilbert. It was easier for the children to understand that "title" than to explain physiotherapy to them. So the leader explained that I had come to take care of their aches and pains. We set up a treatment table and I sat in a low chair as the children gathered around curiously. Then the more adventurous began to show me where they "hurt" by pointing, for example at a point on their forearm. I would nod seriously and gently rub the spot for a few seconds and then give a big smile. The child would also give a satisfied smile and turn away only to be replaced by another and yet another as the fun and innocence of the "game" continued.

Then we noticed that while we were surrounded by these little ones, that one of them had climbed up onto the treatment table and was lying there on her back, quietly waiting for us to notice her.

I went over to her and through the interpreter, the supervisor was able to explain if we could check her leg length, then if there was a discrepancy could we "fix" it. Gently we worked through the protocol correcting her ¾ inch difference and releasing her restrictions right up her spine to the base of her skull. It is a very gentle non-invasive procedure and children love it. When I was finished she gave us a whopping, beautiful smile and jumped down from the table, quickly to be replaced by another child, and I spent the rest of my time there working with a succession of these little ones who jumped up on the table. We eventually left exhausted from the heat but genuinely pleased that we had been able to help so many but a little disappointed that we hadn't been able to conduct the study I had intended. We left the city early the next morning and headed a few hundred miles south to our next destination. Several days later we heard from the Kindergarten Supervisor again who told us of what had occurred after we left that day. Apparently, when the day was over and the parents came to pick up their children there were two of the kids we had worked on who greeted their parents loudly when they saw them. The wonder was that these two kids had both been non verbal until that day! . . . There was considerable excitement and celebration as the word of this "miracle" spread quickly through the city and apparently the surrounding districts and the next morning when the supervisor arrived she found many parents lined up around the building who had brought their children to see me, some had travelled far, as the word spread! We had already left town by this time and never were able to return to this city during our time there.

I believe that both of these children had mild to moderate connective tissue (fascia) restrictions in their throat, probably from birth trauma, which released when I gently stretched them and I would love to go back someday and put the "healings" back into the world of rational explanation and away from the "miracle" status it had been given which hopefully would allow me train many others to use the same protocols I applied to similar cases. Take a moment to ponder just how many of these children's (and children everywhere) perspective of their capabilities or lack thereof can be irrevocably changed forever by this kind of help?

Once they believe that miracles are not only possible they are within their grasp they will not make the decision to submerge their true self and can flourish accordingly.

Then there was Lucy! Lucy is a vivacious and intelligent newscaster for a major TV network in Mexico. She came to see me while I was visiting her home city as she had suffered for years from a badly aligned fracture of her big toe. It was a fairly effortless task to mobilise it back into alignment and she left loudly proclaiming of her "miracle" as she danced back to her car! However, the following morning she was still so happy that she put her foot up on the news desk and announced to every one of the "miracle" she had received the day before. Then, unfortunately, she went on to give out the address where I was working that day! Within hours there was a line up of patients around the house and down the street! I worked until close to midnight and we still had to turn dozens of disappointed people away! I had been working for 13 hours straight and was pretty tired. As we left the house a lady who looked like a grandmother came straight up to us and placed a small baby into my arms, asking me please to heal her! I looked down at this beautiful little girl smiling peacefully at me and it was then I noticed that her left arm was missing! My stomach churned as I realised that this grandmother truly did think I could perform miracles and I was about to say "No, I can't help her," when I saw the deep desperation in her eyes. So I found myself doing what anyone of us would do when given a baby to hold. I said, "She is so beautiful. I am honoured that you have allowed me the privilege of holding her. I will always remember her." And I smiled as I handed the child back to her grandmother. Again the peace that comes from these kids suddenly filled me and I knew that I had made the correct decision. This is exactly what the baby had wanted me to do, so that her grandmother may feel at peace! Every word I have spoken here is true and I indeed have never forgotten that beautiful child who is bringing such peace and light to a world that is in such need of love. There was indeed a miracle that night but it all came from a little baby.

I trust that you have enjoyed these stories, have been uplifted and motivated by them, and that you can actually accept them as possible, whereas had you read about them prior to reading the previous chapters you may not have been quite so open to the possibility.

TWELVE

Anyone Can Perform Miracles!

There is nothing magical or miraculous in my work. There are many cases now where my students are creating similar results. You are just as capable of helping others if you come to understand the principles of the Law of Creation and apply protocols such as KCR and Connective Tissue Release should you so choose. Here is one such story.

My next story took place in my native Scotland in 2010 and is proof that my basic work, known as Kinetic Chain Release (KCR), can be successfully, and often spectacularly implemented, by you, the reader, or by anyone with only a simple weekend training workshop. www.kineticchainrelease.com

Scott is a personable, pragmatic and practical individual, an engineer by profession, with no medical background whatsoever, who attended my KCR workshop in western Scotland. He seemed to thoroughly enjoy the course and took copious amounts of notes on all components. A few days later I received a letter from him. He firstly thanked me for presenting the protocol in such a way that he could easily grasp it, even although medicine was not his background. He went on to say that when he returned home in the late afternoon from my workshop; his wife and children had asked him what it was all about. He explained a little about KCR and volunteered to demonstrate it on each of them, which they enthusiastically agreed to allow.

Scott says that his family all seemed to enjoy the process and were extremely relaxed afterwards. The next thing he became aware of was how they all stayed together for the rest of the evening. If one of them went into the kitchen, then everyone seemed to gravitate there. He said this was most unusual as normally someone is texting, someone else is watching television, etc., but on this night everything just seemed to flow as a peaceful family unit. The following morning as Scott and his wife lay in bed they were joined by their 4 year old son and they engaged in normal early morning Parents and Young Child Dialogue. Several minutes of talking together passed and then the parents gradually came to realize that their son was talking without a stutter! He had always demonstrated difficulty with certain letters and, on this morning, there was no evidence of it whatsoever!

Scott suddenly remembered my teaching of the mother/child connection in the workshop and, as his four year old had not had KCR the evening before, and his wife had, he feels certain that this is in fact what had happened. He told me that should his sons stutter begin to reoccur he would simply perform KCR again on his wife!!

Again a child (and his parents) whose self esteem is threatened by a perceived impediment can confidently believe in miracles and create accordingly.

THIRTEEN

ADD/ADHD/SOCIALLY INEPT/ or Simply an Easily Correctable Physical Restriction

Another beautiful story from a Canadian mother of her 9 year old child's healing, which at one time would have been thought of as miraculous (and according to most western medicine culture still would be) and yet as you are now beginning to understand, the methodologies applied are simple, logical and sequential. There is nothing here that can't be learned.

My beautiful and absolutely delightful 9 year old daughter was diagnosed with Vision Tracking problems (lazy eye) due to what we had been told was "weak muscles" in her eyes approximately 2 years ago. It was an answer I had been searching for. It was an explanation to what had been going with her.

Her symptoms, to name a few, were, she was unable to sit still for any period of time at home or in school, her concentration span was extremely limited, she was frequently and consistently disruptive in class, her reading was way behind other children her age and although she could fully understand the meaning of what was being said or read to her, she was not able to follow along visually. She would compensate by guessing or skipping over sentences altogether.

I had one teacher suggest she had ADHD and suggest medication (her doctor put this theory to rest quickly). This absolutely horrified me. I refused to accept their opinions and began to seek solutions elsewhere. I started with getting her abilities tested through a learning center and it was there that the woman whom I am grateful for noticed that when she read her eyes bounced and flickered. She then told me that this was a sign of tracking issues and suggested she get tested. First she had to go through an eye exam with a certified Optometrist who specialized in this as not all of them do and he agreed that this was the issue.

Then, my partner suggested we try KCR and connective tissue release with Hugh in November 2011. She was extremely shy at first but very quickly she took to Hugh and with her second treatment she was so excited to go she was telling me, "Mommy this makes me feel better."

Since she has been seeing Hugh now for only 3 treatments in a six month period the dramatic improvement is obvious:

Her eyes no longer become sore when reading; Her hand eye coordination has drastically improved; She is able to sit still and concentrate on tasks such as coloring and writing for hours on end; in truth She Has Blossomed! Her grades at school have also dramatically improved.

I definitely credit KCR, CTR and Hugh with solving her problem and also the multiple symptoms that came along with it Also what made me very happy is that this is a practical, mainstream based yet also a holistic approach to health, no medication involved till now and medication will now never need to be involved.

With thanks to Hugh and his work, I pray this will give other parents hope and to help them know that there are indeed miracles out there for their children beyond medications and to help them in the prevention of or removal of the labels that are so easily put upon our children."

It is a good feeling when you know that you have just restored much more than a visual problem in a child. You have restored his or her self esteem before she heaps the evidence of her being a lesser being on herself and begins to immediately utilize the Law of Creation accordingly.

FOURTEEN

Finding My Way Home

"No one saves but ourselves.
 No one can and no one may.
  We Ourselves Must Walk The Path."
   ~ Buddha

Just what did it take to allow me not only to see where I had made the pivotal decision in my life but to begin to repair the damage caused by that decision and to accept and manifest the truths I had known all along? My disconnection from schoolwork caused me to leave school eventually with only minimum passes in 4 subjects. Years before I had passed my mensa tests with flying colors and the future looked bright indeed. Yet here I was, delighted to be out of school yet with terribly limited career options. I chose physiotherapy back then as the idea of being a physical therapist to a professional football (soccer) team seemed like an exciting path to follow. I never truly had been drawn to the path of the priesthood which would have been in the family tradition.

I was now old enough to drink alcohol and my weekends were spent in party mode, although the volume of drink I could consume was subtly and scarily rising. While usually an amenable young guy, when alcohol was in control my submerged anger of many years began to flicker and manifest ominously. Now when challenged, I fought back. On the surface I seemed far from a fighter, much more a lover (well it was the sixties) however inwardly I loved the rock group Sweet's epic "Ballroom Blitz" and somewhat eagerly awaited such scenarios but, when challenged, I fought with such a reckless rage that it scared me. I literally felt no pain in these scenarios, despite being punched, kicked, knifed in the back, metal pipes smashed onto my skull, 5 foot long heavy metal street water keys driven into my shoulder to my lung and slashed with broken glass, and so I withdrew from these challenges, again afraid, although now the fear was, that if I actually unleashed my pent up anger that I may indeed be a threat to my opponents life!

So life went on, I graduated as a Physical Therapist, married a wonderful Glasgow girl and with 2 fine sons (followed by a third) left for a better life in Canada. But, as a friend once told me, no matter where you go, there you are! The drinking on weekends continued as the norm and despite an outwardly happy and successful life the anger was forcing its way through in ever increasing examples.

Suffice to say that my journey back to my real self began 30 years ago with a book, which I will discuss in a later chapter, that would change my life. As I allowed myself to be more in Hakalau I very reluctantly realized in my spiritual "enlightenment" and my self-satisfying "victimhood" that I had actually in many ways become the cowardly angry bully persona that I despised!

This understanding completely shattered me and for a while led to more alcohol. Eventually, after divorce and alienation from my children; followed within 9 years by a second divorce and the loss of almost every penny I owned (this is not a criticism of my ex spouses in any way). I was in situations like being in a hotel room on Christmas day alone, looking out at the massive car park in which mine was the only vehicle . . . or living in a 5 foot by 12 foot bedroom in rented dockside accommodation with paper thin walls and no home to go back to . . . the memories of the boyhood trauma, and my current apparent failures now flooding in so clearly. In the apparent hopelessness of the never ending emptiness inside, suicide was an option I considered and came all too close to several times as still I raged at the world but in reality at myself. I thought I would never heal, that the pain would never end, while outwardly appearing to be upbeat and optimistic, I quite simply didn't want to be around on this planet anymore .

I had spent all of my youth and young adulthood focusing on surviving the multiple occasions where I appeared to be "victimized" . . . of course knowing now that energy flows where attention goes, I was simply and assuredly creating more of the same in ever increasing magnitude.

I see now that the focal point should have been on that boyhood decision to ignore the reality being presented to me so many years ago, and that in reality all I had to do was understand and reverse that decision and everything would change.

I had nothing to lose (actually I had everything to lose). I guess I truly was at the bottom with nowhere else to go. Finally, one night, in what felt like total and overwhelming despair, very close to leaving this world to get rid of the chaos of it all, I heard myself asking God to please take it away or take me back home (whatever that meant). I think I fell asleep instantly and awakened some ten hours later, feeling strangely at peace and bewildered that the anguish I was in had gone! I had asked for it, released all resistance to receiving it and instantly it transpired! and, even for a short time gave me relief and hope. So, with no other options, I began to once again consider "What if" my thoughts of a different life were indeed possible? "What if" I COULD see all the places of my boyhood dreams? "What if" we were ALL capable of performing miracles? "What if" that young boy who survived the self created scenarios of pain and unworthiness for himself and for others, was actually a hero for simply surviving to get to this moment? I began to dream again and slowly, at first, taking things one day or even one minute at a time, then accelerating quickly, everything I had ever wanted to manifest began to appear and still does to this day.

I ask for no sympathy or praise nor condemnation or judgment on any of my story, as it is simply that: My Story—neither good nor bad, just the way it evolved. I do however deeply regret the pain I must have caused others along the way and "I'm Sorry, Please Forgive Me, I Love You, Thank You," is all I can or should say.

No one reading this has to take the tortuous path I subconsciously chose, although I know that many of you have in one way or another. It does not have to take 20 to 40 years to recover. Simply recognize the Law of Creation and begin to recreate your belief in yourself from this moment on.

FIFTEEN

Going Home to California (part one)

A lesson for us all. Curt is a bear of a man in stature. Not overly tall, yet broad shouldered and barrel-chested with thick hands and forearms. An avid biker for many years; a man of many amazing talents and a multi checkered, fascinating life path, he made no claims outwardly of being spiritual, yet clearly is the guardian for his wife, his gentle and deeply spiritual life companion.

On a balmy, windless, perfect evening in Hawaii we were sharing tales of each other's life adventures and he told me of the time when he tried to heal old family wounds and visit his parents in Southern California some years back.

He recalled his leaving home at an early age to embark on an adventure filled path and also to escape the pains of a dysfunctional childhood. Now, years later he is riding his Harley Davidson Motorcycle down through California to his childhood home, determined to find a way to heal the wounds and begin a healthy reconnection process with his now aging parents. He knew that this had to be done for his own peace of mind and spirit and many memories flooded his awareness as the old fears and pain resurfaced, and in some ways he realized just how deeply he had hated this place which was now only hours away as he sped down the Pacific Coast Highway in the warmth of the early morning sunlight.

It was early afternoon when he finally dismounted in front of the scene of some of his earliest traumas. He had not notified his folks that he was coming . . . he figured it was better just to show up without any fanfare or drama. Walking up the path to the front door he was almost overwhelmed as all of the reasons why he left so many years ago returned vividly and seemingly all at once. "God I hate this place!" he said quietly through clenched teeth and, taking a deep breath, he pressed the doorbell and heard the old familiar chime within the hallway. Seconds dragged into a minute or more with no response; he rang again, and a minute later yet again and still the door remained closed to him. Curt was aware of the stillness all around him, it was as though the universe was holding its breath in anticipation, but gradually he realized that the house was empty, no one was home. This confused him as he knew it was Sunday and, as his brother had kept him informed, his parents almost always spent that day at home relaxing and maybe gardening. However, they sure weren't here now, so Curt decided to cruise around for a while and come back in the early evening.

He rode his Harley leisurely down the Coast Highway, enjoying the freedom of the open road, with the sparkling Pacific always close to his right side, until he came to San Juan Capistrano where he sat by the ocean at the beautiful harbor of Dana Point for a while until the sun began to drop towards the horizon. As the shadows lengthened, he returned by the same route until almost at sunset he once again stood at the doorway to his childhood home. Again he rang and again no one answered. After several more tries with no response he realized that no one was there and all of his pent up anger seemed to surface.

"GOD, I HATE THIS PLACE!" he yelled before striding down the path, mounting his motorcycle, accelerating loudly away and driving recklessly north for hours in the moonlight to eventually return, frustrated and exhausted to his apartment some 200 miles away.

He told me that he felt that the message was clear, that he obviously wasn't meant to make peace with his parents and had never returned since that day some 20 years ago.

I waited until he had time to reflect on his words then I said "Perhaps there was another reason they weren't home Curt."

He raised an enquiring eyebrow and waited for my thoughts.

"How do you feel about that place Curt?" I asked.

"I Hate That Place!! . . . I already told you," he said somewhat impatiently.

"And I hear you Curt, however, now let me ask you, what harm did the land itself ever do you? I think that maybe your parents weren't supposed to be there. I think that maybe you were there to make your peace with the land itself!"

After a minute or two of quiet reflection I continued,

"Everywhere I go, Curt, I hear people say they hate this place or that place, whether it's a place where they suffered or a country they feel threatened by. How many people say I Hate America, or Iran or Israel or elsewhere or cannot return to a place such as their hometown or a battlefield because they hate it? Just how massive IS the amount of hate being collectively directed at our life giving planet every day?"

The land where you were raised did nothing wrong, it simply held the energy of what happened there, yet it is the object of your hate! I think you were given the opportunity to return in solitude and reconnect to that beautiful spot. All you had to do was say the words, "I'm Sorry, Please Forgive Me, I Love You, Thank You," to the land and your reconnection would be complete. Think how much vibration of hate is being directed towards the land around the world, and she, the loving force that's supports all life, that we call Mother Earth, has done nothing to deserve such pain.

What do you think would happen if we could all acknowledge this truth and make our peace with the land wherever appropriate? I believe that the collective prayers of reconciliation and reconnection with the land would move humanity forward in a quantum shift to a new global understanding. I truly believe it can be, and is, that simple."

Curt's eyes were misty as he quietly agreed that he had never seen things from that perspective before, but it resonated deeply with him. As we sat in silence, the night smells of perfumed plants filling the warm night air, I felt him come into a deeply rooted sense of peace and I knew he had just truly reconnected with the beautiful land of his childhood and would never feel disconnected from her again.

SIXTEEN

Going Home to California (part two)

So, for all of us who feel anger, rage, shame, guilt or fear when we think of a particularly stressful time of our life, realize that the land itself did nothing wrong except to hold the energetic emotional memory of the event(s) that unfolded upon her. It is the vibration of that energy you feel when you return in thought or physically to that place. So you can rightly say "I hate the emotional energy held in that spot, but I DON'T hate the spot itself!" Making this statement is the beginning of your personal healing.

Then, in recognition of this, take a few deep breaths while imagining what the place you "hate" must have felt like before you came there. If the land is currently holding the energy of what happened to you, imagine what type of energy it was holding in a more peaceful natural time. Imagine how that must have felt, and, as you feel the peacefulness and relaxation of this previous energy, come to realize that there is no reason to hate the land itself, and that you genuinely should say sorry to the land and try to return the energy to what it was before. You do this by sending love instead of hate to that spot and the land will begin to accumulate the love you send and release the previous energy of all the hate you have been sending. Simply feel the beautiful energy of the land the way it used to be and the way you wish it to be again, then say "I'm sorry, Please Forgive Me, I Love You, Thank You," every time you think of her and both you and her will return to the peace which is your natural birthright.

Over time however, I have come to understand that there is yet another VITAL component of healing which, in my experience, is rarely considered or dealt with.

Curt had come to peace with the land and was clearly relaxed, in fact predictably exhausted from finally having released all of his pent up resentment towards the place of his negative experiences. However, when I met him again, some months later, I could clearly see that he was still disconnected energetically and still suffering from the PTSD (Post Traumatic Stress Disorder) from his past experiences. I realized in that moment exactly what and where the missing component was! It all made sense. I have been blessed to have known many men and women whose courage in dealing with their PTSD is truly inspirational, yet my heart has always gone out to them, wishing I could help somehow be of better assistance to them.

As I watched Curt's internal struggles continue I again resonated with the song which has almost become the Vietnam Veterans Anthem, U2's "I Still Haven't Found What I'm Looking For" . . . and this is now 45 years post conflict!!

So let's finish the journey now. As you clear the conflict between yourself and the land you will gradually come to see something else there. It will appear as a light shadow on the ground, or you may gradually notice a small child there, shaking with fear and sadness, probably partially hidden in the scene. That shadow, that child, is you. You see, when we suffer severe trauma, I now believe that a part of our soul/spirit disconnects from us and stays trapped or "frozen" in that place. So every time we refuse to think of that place we are deliberating isolating a very sensitive part of ourselves! . . . and we wonder why we still haven't found what we're looking for!

Even sadder is the thought that every time we say "I Hate That Place," we are sending that hate to the vulnerable disconnected part of ourselves which is lying lonely and forgotten on the ground!

So, when you have made peace with the land and seen yourself there then you recognize the part of you that you have been searching for and you say "I'm Sorry, Please Forgive Me, I Love You, Thank You," and then with all of the compassion you have, please say the words

"Welcome Home!" . . . May you and all of the missing parts of your soul/spirit be reunited now and forever.

Some have said at this point "Now, finally I can close the book on it all."

I say "No, now, finally you can truly begin to heal."
I pray that Curt is finally and swiftly now beginning to heal.
Aloha.

SEVENTEEN

Sticks and Stones . . .

We have no true idea of the ripple effects of our actions otherwise we would behave very differently most of the time. I have come to receive many letters such as the one below simply from believing in the perfection of others and seeing that perfection often buried so deep inside. I easily recognize young people who have made the decision to bury their identity and simply let them feel that there is a better way to move forward. Knowing that someone believes in them is all they need. However, they have such an in- built radar which monitors bullshit! . . . If you tell them that you see their perfection and potential but don't genuinely feel it, they will reject you, often out of hand.

They, like each of you, are incredibly compassionate, gifted, intelligent, fun loving, integrous beings with much to offer society and simply want all of us to see it in ourselves and in each other.

This particular young woman was in a lot of emotional turmoil when I was blessed with meeting her. Forced to bury her true potential at an early age the price she was paying for persisting in this decision was high indeed.

All I did in essence was to see or sense her true essence and recognize my own and the feeling of deep peace flooded in to me again.

Now she is a teacher and mentor to special needs children, and her classroom radiates such peace that other teachers often come there just to sit quietly and enjoy it. She invited me to spend a morning there and that in itself is a gift I will always treasure. She has incorporated yoga, tai chi and healing touch into her curriculum and the children's peaceful and loving response will shape their lives. Her letter to me is a testament, not to me, but to the power of seeing behind the mask these young ones have had to create. How many of us recognize that feeling of separation in ourselves and how quickly can it dissolve if given the chance?

The answer is, almost instantly.

Here are her words of gratitude:

"Dearest Hugh,
There is so much I want to share.
You helped me to change my life.
You were my key influence to stop living a drug addicted depressed life.
You inspired me to follow my dreams.
You showed me that I am worthy. That I am loved.
You helped me to learn that I DO belong on this earth.
You helped me find my inner strength and love.
You gave me the opportunity to share my skills with others.
You inspired me to write a book!
You helped me to dig and push out all of the garbage I have been holding on to and make room to be revitalized and full of love, light, joy and compassion.
I see the world with clearer eyes. I can live with love and am learning to live without judgement.
You started my path of healing and because of that foundation you instilled, I continue to grow and embrace life in the present moment.
You are such a gift to the children of the earth.
You show us the way.
I love you completely and deeply."

So, if we recognize the power of our words and even the energy of our thoughts, and thus our judgments, when dealing with anyone, but particularly with children (and with ourselves!) we can knowingly or unknowingly direct them and us into creating a hell on earth or we can allow them and us to create (Law of Creation) a Heaven on earth. It IS up to you.

"Sticks and Stones May Break My Bones but Names Will Never Hurt Me," this childhood mantra is another deeply and deliberately implanted example of "The Lies That Bind." For the truth has always been "Sticks and Stones May Break My Bones but words Will Break My Heart" . . . Please memorize this phrase and consider it deeply.

The words which we say to ourselves can be just as destructive as those we say to others. We all know that telling ourselves how stupid or ugly we are is destructive but sometimes it can be more subtle.

I was seeing patients on the Luxury resorts of Jalisco when a European billionaire came to see me. He had said it was for treatment to his shoulder, but he hadn't wanted to say why he was actually coming. After the initial pleasantries, I asked him how I could help him? I was slightly taken aback when, after a moment's hesitation, he asked me why he was unhappy!

I asked him to explain further, and he told me that he was confused. He said he had even taken to saying a mantra 100 times each morning and evening but still he could not relax.

Now this is a self made billionaire, an astute and intelligent individual, who had his massive yacht, complete with helicopter on board, awaiting him in the harbor. So I asked him what was the mantra he was using? He replied "No Worry, No Stress, No Worry, No Stress" "I say that aloud every morning and evening to set my intent and all I get is worry and stress! Please help me Hugh."

I simply said "My friend, what happens if I ask you repeatedly not to think of a pink elephant?" He looked positively stunned as he realized how his words were actually working against him. If he had said words like Peace and Harmony guess what he would have been experiencing?

A shocking example of how this form of psychology is deliberately used to hurt children springs into my memory now. We were a class of 12 year old boys in the aforementioned Roman Catholic environment. One week the Foreign Missionary Priests came to see us. This was an annual event where we sat and were lectured by these well trained individuals. Unfortunately I hesitate to say well meaning. Take a second now and remember "Don't Think Of A Pink Elephant!" . . . So, this priest tells us (almost shouting at us) that thinking of a naked woman is evil—deeply evil—mortal sin evil!! . . . that EVEN ONE THOUGHT of a naked woman would condemn us to Hell for all eternity! . . . "SO DO NOT EVER EVER THINK OF A NAKED WOMAN," he thundered. . . . Of course we were all instantly sent to hell and could not stop thinking of naked women!! . . . Imagine the guilt deliberately inflicted on innocent children by this cruel and vicious indoctrination. The ramifications throughout their lives would be many indeed.

May we all in this moment see through all of the deliberate lies that each of us has been told and remember our innocence and our perfection.

In a universe where everything truly is possible, the word NO does not exist. How many times do we tell young children "Do NOT touch that," and they immediately touch it! There is no "NO" in the universe. Don't make the same mistakes with this in your life. For example, I first landed on Hawaii when I was 39 years old and fell in love with it instantly. I returned several times in quick succession, then determined somehow to move there, and my mantra became "I will NOT wait till I'm 65 to get down here." Guess what happened! I was finally able to go there for 3 months at a stretch, and guess what age I was? 65! Point taken?

Another misuse of words is one which deeply affects many of today's children. It is the misuse of the word WEIRD. How many times do we hear kids say that a particular topic is "just weird" or, alternatively, say "I just can't learn that stuff. It's just weird." Well apparently science has now proven that thinking something is weird actually partially shuts down the left or rationale thinking side of the brain! This part of the brain naturally logical will not tend to associate itself with anything deemed to be weird. If, instead of weird, a child can be taught to say something along the lines of "I just can't seem to learn that. It's kind of fascinating actually!" then the child's brain actually kicks in to increased activity and begins to solve the problem before it, often with astonishing results. Another example of the role and power of words.

Recall how I began this chapter by stating that words alone are not enough. You have to be able to recognize the perfection and potential in another before saying the words to young people or they will see them for the platitudes they are and probably not listen to you again. Now listen to these words to live by. There was a survivor of the death camp at Auschwitz in WWII who was asked how he felt about the guards and Gestapo there, he replied "They tried their best to make me hate them, and they failed. If I had hated them I would have become just like them." And then the big one "If they could see the light in them that I can see, they would not behave the way that they do." This was truly an extraordinary man, who hit the nail on the head. If we can just see the light in others, despite their resistance, they will shift. Somehow this man survived by staying in a state of love and compassion and not succumbing to the fear and horror surrounding him. Who knows what other good his love of others achieved as you can guarantee that his true connection to the guards made a difference to others on multiple occasions.

So often if we are hurt by another, we are torn between feelings of hating them, yet still, on another level, unable to stop loving them. How many of us feel that way about previous relationships that have ended painfully?

If you look for the light inside of those people from our past, or even the present, you will see that this is the part of them that you love. This is the part of them which they cannot see in themselves. This is their authentic self that they have forgotten. It is their behavior that is unacceptable to you. It is their behavior that you hate!

So, in effect, I could say to a "terrorist" and mean it sincerely "I love you and always will. However I hate your behavior and will not tolerate them." That way the problem is clearly identified as another's behavior and the problem of changing that is completely up to them and frees you forever.

So now let's get back to today's children and young adults. As the story at the start of this chapter clearly demonstrates, all they need is for someone to see and connect to the god given perfection within them and their behavior often change instantly! Maybe that's all any of us need.

EIGHTEEN

Party Time! The Proof That Dreams DO Come True, and We DO Create!

This is the absolute proof you have been waiting for. If you are not yet totally convinced of your potential, read on, every word is true.

This is my story of how an exercise to teach relaxation manifested in every detail over four years later and I truly became free for the first time and could clearly begin to see and celebrate that my childhood dreams of all of our unlimited human potential were correct. "The Lies That Bind" were still strong however and have taken me on a very winding path since that time to the full realization and acceptance of our individual and collective capabilities. Please put the lies aside and allow yourself to be totally immersed in this truth and it will save you from the loss of years that I still manifested as my resistance slowly diminished.

I was in Beautiful British Columbia attending an 8 day Hospital Departmental Management Certification workshop, surrounded by the breathtaking scenery of the ocean and the mountains, pinching myself, in gratitude that I was actually there, as I have done in so many places.

I had just attended one of the workshops and was musing over what had happened there.

The lecturer was giving a talk on the benefits of meditation for stress reduction in business.

Her talk honestly didn't resonate with me as she spoke but I really had no feelings one way or another about it. What shocked me was the reaction from the audience when individuals told her that they objected to voodoo talk such as this at a mainstream conference, while others

ANGRILY told her she was anti Christian! I couldn't believe their rudeness nor begin to imagine just what she had said that could stir such fear and antagonism. The poor woman was clearly shaken by the response to her offering. She had recommended some reading material, namely *The Aquarian Conspiracy* by Marilyn Ferguson. Still pondering what I had witnessed I wandered into the UBC Bookstore and there, front and centre, at eye level was *The Aquarian Conspiracy* . . . "OK then," I mused. "This is the recommended reading and it is here in major mainstream university bookstore so it must have SOME merit. I don't have to like it, but I should give it a fair chance." So there and then I purchased a copy and returned to my room to see what the fuss could possibly be about.

Marilyn's views actually made sense as I absorbed them. Meditating seemed as though it actually might quieten and clear my mind so I may achieve my goals in business so I decided to try one of the simple ones she recommended, just to see if it had merit.

In essence, each night before drifting off to sleep I had to create a place where I was at perfect peace. It had to be a place where I had been before. Then when I was aware of every last detail, sound and smell, I had to visualize turning around and doing the same thing until finally able to look in any one direction and know exactly what was all around me in all directions, feeling at perfect peace with it all. This process probably took me over a month to master. Then the next part of the meditation could be implemented. In that perfect scenario I had created I now had to place someone I had never seen before there with me. I had to trust this person unconditionally and still feel at peace and had to keep changing the person's appearance/persona until everything blended perfectly.

I was happy to go along with it as I was beginning to enjoy drifting off to sleep each night peacefully without mentally planning my next day's activities or reviewing my career goals.

Finally I was able to share my imaginary space with a stranger I trusted completely. That is where the last part of the meditation was to be implemented.

Ask the person a question! . . . This was the end of the road for me. I went blank and could think of absolutely nothing to say . . . my vision dissolved instantly and I never was able to recreate it again, gradually forgetting all about it completely.

Now fast forward a few years. I am the Manager/Coach of the University of Lethbridge Men's Football (soccer) team. One day I received an invitation to bring my team down to play in Hawaii at Christmas! I told the players about it at a team meeting and also that, if we were to get there we would have to raise the money ourselves as there would be no school funding available for such a venture. My team laughed at the prospect as it would require fundraising of over $20,000 in a few short months (this would equate to over $60,000 in today's economy). I told them to keep the faith and let's just go for it and five months later we were a group of twenty winging our way to Big Island for 2 weeks with all expenses raised and covered.

I had always dreamed of Hawaii as one of my magical places I would see someday, although having absolutely no idea how it could evolve, so I had to pinch myself often in amazement as we stepped down from the aircraft in Kona, feeling the gentle tropical night breeze and smelling the strong and sweet perfumes of the abundant natural flora and fauna. It was New Year's Eve and just two hours later we were toasting each other's health by the ocean as the fireworks crackling and glittering around the harbor illuminated the water in a rainbow of color and somehow seeming to welcome our arrival as well as the coming year.

We had a wondrous time indeed while there, which does not require elaboration in this story, however, there was one day which would impact my life forever.

I was lost in the knowledge that yet another part of my childhood "dreams" had come true and was savoring every second of it. On this particular day we were all at a local beach called Hapuna; once rated as one of the top ten most beautiful on the planet. I was floating around just outside of the mild surf break line and decided to swim leisurely down the full around 800 meters length of the beach. I swam casually totally luxuriating in this tropical paradise and laughing inwardly at the thought of the Canadian winter manifesting fiercely back in Lethbridge. Reaching the far end I allowed the waves to bring me in and gently deposit me on the sand at the north end of the beach. It was so beautiful and peaceful that I felt unbelievably relaxed and calm. A small path wound invitingly up into the trees from the beach so I decided to follow it for a short way to see what was there. I had only gone less than 20 meters when I was stopped in my tracks. I couldn't grasp what I was seeing and feeling. I was in the EXACT spot that I had created in my forgotten meditation over four years previously! I knew that I recognized every tree, every plant, every rock, every smell and every sound in a split second! I knew what was to my left or right before looking. My creation had manifested exactly as I had imagined it to be. For some time I felt flickers of fear that I was actually asleep, dreaming, and would awaken at any moment and find myself back in the middle of blizzard battered Lethbridge! Gradually the fear subsided and I began to relax and accept where I was, still mystified by it all but completely at peace within the experience. I have no concept of how long I stayed there but finally I decided it was time to go and resolved to return every day until we flew home.

Feeling incredibly serene I returned through the trees to the beach and decided to walk along the edge of the ocean with the warm water lapping slowly and rhythmically over my ankles. As I began back towards the south end of the beach I became aware of a man walking towards me, also clearly enjoying the Aloha of his vacation. We smiled and nodded a silent greeting to each other as we passed. Then, yet again I was stopped in my tracks as I realized that the man I has just nodded to was the man I had created in such great detail in my meditation!

Even more confused than ever I turned around to see him and he was gone, I assumed he had followed the same path I had just come from. Determined to at least introduce myself I walked quickly back up the path but never did see him again even although I returned for the next six days and again when I returned with my spouse one year later for a two week vacation which in reality was more of a personal quest for me.

Within a couple of years my manifested spot was obliterated by construction equipment and a resort hotel now stands on the ground I once knew so well. So, once again the memories and their importance gradually slipped away from my consciousness until it no longer factored in my world.

Fast forward again another twelve years. I am a physical therapist, in private practice in Calgary. I had built a very successful business and my clinic was seeing over 80 clients per day. Our results were outstanding and the new referrals were steady. I had developed a simple system of rebalancing the human body, which I had named Kinetic Chain Release (KCR) TM and the recovery time of almost all of our patients was far outstripping the vast majority of our competitors, not just locally but nationally and even Internationally, thanks for the most part to KCR. Never one to sit on my laurels I then focused on finding out how it could all be improved even further and spent three years studying Occupational Health stresses, analysis of job descriptions and work site analysis, work injuries, safety issues and injury reduction programs etc.

There was a deep knowing inside me that there had to be something more (isn't there always?). Something I needed to complete the puzzle I was trying to solve.

One day a brochure came in the mail to my office. It was a standard mail out extolling the merits of something called Myofascial Release. I had never heard of it, Myofascia, otherwise known as Connective Tissue was barely touched upon in my training and was not given any recognition in medical schools anywhere in the Western world. I almost put it into the garbage there and then, but suddenly was drawn to the graphics of the handout. They were very eye catching as intended and there was a sketch of the presenter of this series of workshops, a fellow physical therapist by the name of John Barnes. Memories of Hawaii flooded back to me, as clear as if they were only yesterday as I realized that I was again looking at the person I had "created" in my meditation almost eighteen years previously!

There was no question I had for him back then at Hapuna but clearly I had questions now.

Within the hour I had booked my flights and my hotel to into his next series of workshops to begin in Atlanta, Georgia within the next few days, Suffice to say this work was indeed my missing link to my work and over the following two years I was blessed to get to know John and his groundbreaking work well and, in that time, attended all twelve or thirteen of his courses, expanding my awareness of the human body beyond belief and in its application along with KCR, providing even more spectacular results in resolving physical issues with patients globally, often thought of and celebrated as "miracles" by them as they had given up all hope of being "cured" from their afflictions.

If you do not yet believe that I indeed manifested all of the above then I suggest you read it over again. There is no other possible explanation. In my meditation I had, with no inner resistance (and that was the secret) created a perfect place with the perfect teacher I would need when the time was right and it manifested in sequence exactly when I needed it.

Therefore there is nothing preventing you from creating anything you truly desire. You simply have to FEEL how good it will feel when it manifests, with no doubt in your heart that it will. Do this as often as you can and your future is most definitely assured.

NINETEEN

"The Universe is in perfect order, the ONLY chaos is in our minds." ~ John F. Barnes, P.T.

[The second that we finally realize this, then our journey becomes one of wonder and prosperity.]

I will give you one more fascinating true example now of how belief systems can be shifted in an instant. This story should give you any further proof you require, however, if you still haven't gotten the point, don't worry I won't give up on you but will offer you other methodology, which I'll address later in the book. For now, just relax and enjoy Laura's tale.

Firstly, let me ask you the question "Are You Perfect?" Most people immediately answer a definite "No, Of Course Not" and there begins the problem. Many others say "Of Course I am" but the life they lead tells that inwardly they really don't quite believe that to be true.

For those of you who have already realized this truth, simply enjoy this reinforcement.

This is an astonishing story of courage and ultimate triumph. Laura is a truly bright spirited, compassionate lady who came into my life over ten years ago now for treatment to her chronic neck and her debilitating severe head pain which she had suffered with for over eight years. She had a medical history of substance abuse, following an abusive childhood (anyone realize yet how she had manifested it all subconsciously?). Laura had fought to overcome her addictions successfully and held a position in the airline industry and was married and was also doing an excellent job of running her household and raising her children. Her parents were estranged and had little contact with her on any real level. The physical pain in her face was massive and constant to the point where it seemed that no one believed her any more. Due to the legalities and her confidentiality I will not elaborate further, suffice to say we found the cause of her pain, a foreign body that had been left inside her following surgery, which appeared to be an open and shut case of extreme medical negligence, as she now had the foreign object in question to show the world. On her recovery, extremely angry at the way she had been treated and misdiagnosed over the years, she sued the system and despite overwhelming evidence (and I do mean overwhelming) in her favor, her case was eventually, and stunningly, thrown out of court. She did not receive a dime in compensation, complicated by the fact that she has spent her life savings on legal costs.

Her facial pain however was completely resolved although she still attended me once week to help eliminate the cumulative damage that had been done to her connective tissue in her neck and shoulders due to her pre existing medical condition.

As she lay quietly face up, eyes closed, on my treatment table I found myself beginning to give her the following story. I quietly asked her if she was perfect, as I sat at the head of the treatment table with her head resting gently in my cupped hands. Laughingly she replied "Of Course Not, Hugh."

And so I said, "Just consider this for a moment. Do you know what the Hubble Telescope is Laura?" She nodded in agreement that she knew of the wondrous space telescope hurtling through the galaxy sending a constant stream of stunning pictures back to earth daily. "Laura, have you ever looked at the images it is sending back?" I continued. She gently shook her head in a negative response.

"Think of it this way," I said next. "Up until very recent times we, the general public had little or no idea just how amazing the skies above us are. We knew about our few planets and had heard of the Milky Way, but other than that, it was unquestionably a kind of 'Twinkle, Twinkle Little Star' or a 'Somewhere Over The Rainbow' concept in the main to most of us. Then along comes this explosion of science and up goes the Hubble sending pictures back into our homes via the wonder of the Internet. Stunning really when you think about it! So I want you to go onto your laptop when you go home today Laura and to check out the top ten pictures from the Hubble. Their clarity and color will amaze you as you begin to understand just a small portion of the beautiful vastness that is beyond our earthly eyes. You will look in wonder and I guarantee that at one particular one you will almost be overcome by its beauty and its absolute perfection, causing you to say the words Oh My God aloud. It is in this moment, seeing pictures unavailable to mankind until now, that you will know without a doubt that there is a higher intelligence, call it what you will or not at all, somehow behind it all and that it is all unfolding just perfectly."

"So, with that inner knowing Laura that it is all perfect, does it make any sense to think that you, a microdot of a specimen in it all, on a microdot of a planet could be the creator's mistake? If you doubt what I say, ignore my words, go back to the Hubble, and start again. It will eventually hit you, I promise."

Laura seemed to be barely breathing as she rested, listening to my words and I suspect imagining what I spoke of.

"What if the real ego would be to think that you are NOT perfect? That you in effect are this higher intelligence's mistake and one that cannot be fixed? What if what they have taught you about your imperfection was another of 'The Lies That Bind'?"

"I believe that everything is about energy Laura, and thankfully even the science of today agrees with me. You can think of it as energy, light or love, it's all the same thing and I believe that this energy is the force that drives the universe. I believe that if you send out energy/light/love by your words, thoughts or actions, that the universe will send it back to you multiplied many times over. So here it comes Laura, gift wrapped packages of prosperity from the universe all around you, but you won't open them and never have because you believe you are imperfect and unworthy of such gifts. The universal intelligence of course couldn't care less whether you open them or not, it is simply the universe being the universe and doesn't attach to your perceptions in any way as you indeed have free will."

"So," I continued, "what if I'm right? What if it is as simple as accepting these gifts with your next intake of breath? What do you have to lose?"

In response, Laura inhaled deeply and sighed as she exhaled. We didn't mention it again that day.

The following Monday, exactly one week later, Laura returned for her next appointment as scheduled.

My clinical waiting room, as usual at that time of day, was full of patients awaiting treatment from my staff. Most were injured workers from the nearby steel mills and heavy duty industrial surroundings. The banter between them was excellent at these times and we all had to be on our toes to hold our own with them. I saw Laura standing at the front desk and just motioned her to come back through the gymnasium to the cubicled and curtained area along each of its sides.

She didn't respond instead she said clearly "What did you do to me last week?" You could have heard a pin drop as all conversation and all activity on the gym equipment ceased immediately.

"I don't know Laura," I responded. "What DID I do to you last week?"

"I'm not sure," she continued, "but I saw you on the Monday and on the Tuesday I received this!" . . she reached into her coat pocket and produced a letter of some sort and laid it on the counter in front of her. She went on to state that the contents of the letter were in fact from her father who had always given her money whenever things got rough and had always insisted that one day she would have to pay him back. This letter stated that she was formally released from all debt to him and he signed the letter "Love, Dad."

Laura expressed her joy at being released from a lifetime of accumulated debt but was utterly unsure what to do with the ending as she never recalled her father having said those words to her in her childhood.

There was a murmur of support for Laura throughout my clinic as I smiled and again waved her toward me. Again she shook her head saying "No, I'm not done."

A somewhat excited silence had again descended on my facility as we awaited an explanation. Laura reached into her other pocket, producing an even thicker letter and she then placed it on to the counter beside the first one. The day after her father's letter was in her hands this second letter was delivered. It was from her mother. And, in essence it said that she (the Mom) knew she had made many mistakes in Laura's childhood and would she (Laura) please consider starting over?

There was more than a little clearing of throats as the men listening were clearly touched by her story and were trying to desperately initiate conversation lightheartedly again.

For a third time I tried to bring Laura back to me and again she shook her head saying she wasn't finished. She held everyone in the palm of her hand by this time as she began to explain how on the next day after her mother's letter arrived she received a telephone call from the lawyer who was in charge of her case which had only ended a few weeks previously. The lawyer told her that since the previous Monday she could not get Laura out of her head. She had lost nights of sleep reviewing their case and could find no reason as to where they had failed Laura. However for her own peace of mind she was reimbursing Laura fully for all of the retainers she had been paid, in essence Laura's life savings! There was wild applause and laughter at this as Laura somewhat proudly finally walked back to me.

So, in effect Laura had believed in the law of the universe for just one breath and, by instantly releasing all of her previous perceptions, within four days all of her problems resolved.

Within a year she had moved to the Canadian west coast, had a home close to the shore where she can sit and watch the pods of killer whales cruise past her while golden eagles nest in a tree nearby. Her life truly has come full circle and she is an outstanding and glittering example for us all.

The lesson from the Hubble is this.

"The Universe Is In Perfect Order, The ONLY Chaos Is In Our Minds." John F. Barnes, P.T.

The second we realize this, our path becomes one of wonder and prosperity.

Laura has always stayed in touch with me throughout the years and continues to live the life of her dreams.

TWENTY

The Power of Human Touch

We have forgotten the power of the human touch. Many times it's all we need. "The Lies That Bind" have gradually and relentlessly isolated our children and you and I from this most basic human need, and have deliberately created more chaos in our minds and increased the sense of separation in our hearts. In Sweden a few years ago the lack of touch among children was all too apparent and clearly unnatural. So a social experiment, known as "Healing Touch" was initiated in one school, with parental consent, and I believe was implemented by the classes of five to eight year old children.

Every morning to begin the school day the children had to spend approximately ten minutes touching each other! Can you imagine trying to implement this in, for example, some parts of the U.S.A.? There would be outrage in the extreme. All physical contact is banned in many schools there, even children who high five each other have faced disciplinary charges, and woe betide any child who dared to hug another child to comfort them in their fear, pain or sorrow. Our deliberately fear based societal rules and regulations keep us further and further apart from our hearts and consequently from the truth of the Law of Creation. We all need to be aware of this Swedish experiment and ensure it spreads. I have a copy of the program and have left it in Mexico for the native Huichol children and passed it on in Hawaii and Argentina, hoping that it will soon become the norm globally.

Each morning, the children began their day by sitting in a circle each child facing the back of the child sitting in front of them. Children did not have to participate and could sit and just observe if they chose.

After taking a few deep and quieting breaths they began their daily ritual of touching. The teacher would gently say something like "The long green grass swayed back and forward in the gentle warm breeze" or "The falling rain gently pitter pattered onto the warm earth" or "A butterfly flew happily over the fields of flowers" or "Clouds floated across the bright blue sky" or "The sun sleepily began the day by coming up over the hills." The children had to picture the scenes and then, using their fingers, draw them or act them out on the back of the child in front.

The children took to this practice eagerly and they seldom did not all join in the circle. It was noted how much more happy they all appeared to be following this, but that in itself while exciting was still a subjective observation. Then the stunning objective proofs began to present themselves. Over a three month period it was noted that incidents of bullying had not diminished. They had DISAPPEARED COMPLETELY from the focus groups!

Cooperation not competition was now the norm! When a child had difficulty grasping a topic in class, other children would go over to them and help them to understand until they grasped it! Average class grades have risen accordingly.

Can you imagine the feeling of peace and harmony and safety created in these wonderful classrooms by these heroic teachers?

Imagine if bullying became non-existent and cooperation the norm in schools in your area?

It is not the touch that is an issue. It is the INTENT behind the touch or for that matter any action taken by any of us that is important. Children are naturally trusting but we forget they are also naturally perceptive to intent of word or action. They know when a touch or action is made from love or from non love. They can differentiate and respond appropriately if you let them. While we must always be the guardians for our youth we must also allow them to develop their own powers of discernment so they can grow into confident well adjusted adults.

I ask you now to remember the beauty in a loving touch at some time in your life, and if you cannot remember the comfort in this, then follow the children's example and start it with your own children, yes, even the rebellious renegade teenagers, they probably need it the most and will enjoy it despite their protests to the contrary. Families in counseling should have to start each session with ten minutes of healing touch; board room members everywhere should do like-wise before planning their corporate future. This is not an effeminate or weak or a hippie concept as we have been told. This is a most powerful and basic human tool which has gradually been denied to us. It is a tool which produces almost instant results and cannot be overdone.

Children's natural cooperation does not have to be encouraged or created and can be seen everywhere if we open our eyes or, more importantly, our hearts. I remember some twenty years ago, I and my business partners decided to run a "Kids of Steel" Triathlon in Canada. In this mini triathlon 10 to 15 year old kids had to swim, then cycle, then run preset endurance distances consecutively. The idea was received with great enthusiasm and sponsors lined up to help us, the city council agreed to close off the roads to traffic for the duration of the race and entries began to come in from far afield. We were blessed with a sunny spring day for the event. We had a "staggered" start which meant the young ones hit the water first, followed at few minute intervals by the older kids, so that hopefully they could all arrive at the finish line at around the same time. There was a large group of supportive parents and siblings in attendance and the excitement was clearly visible on all of the faces of the participants as they prepared to put their young bodies and spirits to the test. There were participation medals for all, with small trophies for the fastest completion times in each age group The kids fairly drove through the water and eventually raced out of the Olympic sized pool to mount their bicycles and, to the excited applause and cheers of their supporters, pedaled off as hard as they could onto the prescribed route. As they began the third and final leg of the race, the 5km run, you could see the adrenaline was fading for some and fatigue was now becoming a factor as they set off, their initial enthusiasm now replaced by deep determination to finish. It was here that the magic began to unfold for us all.

With two kilometers left many of the younger kids were starting to struggle to keep running. They were so bravely trying to complete the challenge they had undertaken and many a tear rolled reluctantly down their cheeks as they were passed by the older kids coming through from behind. Then one older boy, who was easily passing them all and was clearly set to lift the trophy for best time overall suddenly stopped running!

He began talking to one of the younger kids who was clearly in distress and within a short time they were walking towards the finish line together! Finishing first, for this young man was not as important as helping this little one. His spontaneous example was instantly contagious as other stronger kids began to stop running and to encourage and to help the younger ones proudly finish, to the delight and the tears of the adults assembled at the finish line.

Every child finished the event that day, everyone's self esteem was intact, everyone cherished their medals of achievement, no one felt like a failure and MANY hugs were shared by the kids and adults alike as they all loudly celebrated each other receiving their medals. There was a magic in the air that I can still recall.

The magic of human cooperation and compassion once again proved to be the norm and the chaos in our minds to be the illusion.

What a lovely thought to hold as we end this chapter.

TWENTY ONE

I Stopped Passing the Buck by Passing the Buck!

Each of us is capable of making massive changes to our worlds. It is all too easy to wring our hands and feel helpless to change things or to bury our heads in the sands of our selfishness and pretend all is well, regardless of how our actions or inactions impact others. This story is a case in point.

It was around 1985 or 1986 when the deliberately manipulated Ethiopian Famine and Genocide was at its height. I, like most people was unaware of the political agendas surrounding these horrors and felt rising frustration that there seemed to be nothing that anyone of us could really do to help, except donate to various agencies, with no guarantees that our donations would get to their intended targets. Every night on the news, the stories of thousands upon thousands of innocent families and whole communities starving to death filled our television screens along with continuous pleading for financial aid to send them the food, medicine and shelter they were dying for the lack of. It had been going on for over 2 years and showed no real signs of abating despite a global response on every level. Little did I know that within two weeks I would be brought to truly understand the horror of this carefully orchestrated scenario. One evening while watching the news with my family, as I looked at our dinner table in gratitude, seeing it filling with steaming bowls and plates of food for us all, I suddenly became enraged at the inequality of it all and unable to face the overabundance on my table and still empathize with the starving millions in Ethiopia, I stormed out of my home, into my truck, and disappeared into the open highway in a cloud of dust! I floored the accelerator as I cleared city limits and was soon rocketing west along Highway 1 towards the snow capped Rocky Mountains about 100 kilometers away. My long suffering wife and sons were not overly surprised at my actions as, like I have already described, in those days my anger at feeling helpless was a reminder of childhood scenarios and was all too close to the surface on many occasions. I never asked but I suspect they actually had a most enjoyable, guilt free and peaceful supper due to the fact that I wasn't there.

I inwardly, and in some moments vocally, cursed and raged at the helplessness of it all, and the fact that there seemed to be no way of knowing which of the multiple charitable aid organizations was the best to donate to. It was at best a crap shoot and at worst was a complete waste of resources and we never quite knew which. I realized that the same thing applied on the home front. We were constantly bombarded to donate to various group and had to be selective without actually understanding their worth.

As I finally sat for a long time, as the sun began to set, high on the Rockies on a bluff overlooking the Bow river, just close to the magical town and ski centre we know as Banff, a vague idea began to form somewhere deep below the now gradually subsiding anger. I didn't feel helpless anymore. I had a plan. I drove home calm and focused. One man CAN make a difference. One man WILL make a difference. I will not wait for someone else to make that difference. In this instance that man would be ME. That is all that sustained me throughout those first days.

Just ten days later I was standing in front of a group of people in a rented church hall and, as they gazed at me expectantly, I had no real idea of what I was about to say. However, it all came out of me much better than I had hoped for and what a wonderful time of learning was about to begin.

Before me were assembled representatives from every church and charitable organization who were collecting for Ethiopia that I could find. I had contacted them one by one explaining that as a member of the public, I had no idea where I should entrust my limited availability of finances to ensure it was of maximum benefit. I told them that I had booked a church hall and that I would appreciate their attendance to clarify my confusion, and then I hung up. I thought I would be lucky if one or two showed, but here I was facing representatives from at least a dozen International Aid Organizations!

After I had introduced myself and my agenda, they took it in turns to stand and state who they were and which organization they were representing. I realized that none of them knew each other, even from our small city of around 60,000 people. So, I asked how many of them knew what the others actually did for charity and I think we were all a little stunned when the reality set in that they knew as little about the each other as I did!

So the first order of business was to rectify this and it was agreed that the first step was for each person in the group to present to the rest of us exactly what their mission statement was all about. This would take several weeks of presentations so we booked the same church hall every Wednesday for six weeks to accomplish this mutual understanding. I felt it was imperative to establish this base line before proceeding towards my goal which was now clear, but had not shared as yet. However we were also blessed to have a young physician from "Doctors Without Borders" in attendance and he had just returned from Ethiopia a few days earlier. He gladly took centre stage to somewhat sadly give us his firsthand account of what was happening there. We were mesmerized and quite stunned as he told his story and no one spoke for some time after he had finished.

He painted a picture of how, in all the time he was there he was never allowed any connection with the refugees. All camera equipment was confiscated and he was held within the confines of the capital city of Addis Ababa by an encircling blockade of Russian troops. He told of seeing massive storage dumps of medicine, food and blankets that would never reach their intended recipients, but instead were being put on the black market or shipped to Russia.

He told how these poor people were actually the victims of a controlled genocide; how they had been taken from their mountain villages and towns and deposited in the middle of the desert to die. He told how he personally witnessed occasions when these suffering families actually managed to stagger out of the desert and arrive at Addis Ababa, where they were loaded onto trucks, driven back out deep into the desert and once again abandoned. Their deaths were being used to gather massive injections of money and supplies for the Soviets.

Donating further aid would be of no benefit. Only global intervention (which never came) could help.

Over the next month our group met weekly and gradually came to understand the focus and the working of each other's organizations.

There was truly some heart-warming work going on in the world despite the insanity of action of some world leaders. I remember many of the stories, however one in particular still stands out in my mind for its ultimate success and humor.

There was a village in Kenya that had been selected for aid programs and it had been agreed to set up fresh water well in the village, plus establish a sustainable vegetable garden project and build a schoolhouse. The women walked for five kilometers each day to fetch water and bring it back to the village, which must have been exhausting but a task they performed without complaint. Eventually the new well was drilled in the village and that particular issue was solved. Or so the aid workers thought! The well repeatedly became unusable as wildlife kept falling in and their bloated corpses polluted the water source. No one could figure out why this was happening for many months until one very astute aid worker discovered the problem. She called a meeting of the women in the village to discuss the problem. She asked them, if the freshwater well was moved to around three kilometers from the village did they think that animals might stop falling into it? Smiles and nods of approval surrounded her. The worker realized that the daily walk for water was the women's chance to visit with each other without their men folk around. It was the men who suggested the well be brought into the village, no one had consulted the girls! So this women's liberation action of sabotage resulted in a large well drilled close enough so they wouldn't be overtired yet far enough that they could still enjoy their girl time together! Great Story that one.

It was during these few weeks of exchange between the groups that I unrolled my proposal.

I wanted to get their attention on just two points.

1. Can you imagine what it would be like for the public if just once all of your groups combined into a single cause? . . . This fired their imaginations and I was more than a little surprised at their immediate agreement!

2. Every city in Canada had a "twin" city somewhere in the world, where they exchanged cultural events etc. Why couldn't every city in Canada "adopt" an area on the planet and support aid agencies working there? . . . Again they all were enthused and agreed within minutes!! Game On, I thought, Now to choose an area!

We reviewed all of the work we had been shown in the last few weeks and, for several reasons selected Swaziland. One was that geographically it was similar in size to Southern Alberta where we were based and secondly while the ruling royalty became richer, the rural populations were depleted and neglected. So, Swaziland was unanimously accepted as our focus. The next stage was to determine the real needs of the people there. After the deceptions of Ethiopia we were all skeptical of the propaganda being presented in the mainstream media. Also how could we minimize costs of getting the aid there. I suggested we talk to the men and women on the front lines of poverty in Swaziland. Just a week later I was sitting in our local community college on a radio link to a transmitter deep in the bush of Swaziland and talking to Father Joe, a Franciscan priest who was dedicating his life to helping these people in any way he could. Once he got over the shock of his prayers being answered in this manner he gave us a very practical list of needed materials and programs. We were all genuinely getting the sense that something momentous was unfolding here. We had the idea of all agencies working together; we had the target identified and the principle of communities helping communities clearly defined as another part of the vision. Now all we needed was a name. I went to a local lounge bar and, with a cold beer in front of me began to focus on a name.

I contemplated on how, for every dollar we raised the government had committed to match. I realized that it wouldn't have to break anyone's bank account as long as a lot of people gave even a little … what if everyone just gave a dollar? What if hunger could be solved by just giving a dollar? What if this was the answer to the world poverty issues? . . . Excitedly I decided that our marketing would be that we would only accept donations of one dollar and everyone needed to get involved and stop passing the buck to others!!! And so the foundation of "Pass The Buck" was born over a beer!

We had another meeting, the name was enthusiastically approved and registered and a date for a one day collection blitz was agreed upon. The media embraced the project and I had several interviews with local TV and radio stations as well as the local newspaper. The Lord Mayor of Lethbridge actually handed me a personal cheque for $400 on television and, to his surprise I handed it back as all I needed from him was a dollar. (In retrospect I should have taken it but then 20/20 hindsight is easy for us all) Much help began to arrive as dozens of people came to help organize the day, and then it all actually happened.

At the end of our 4 hour blitz, all groups united as one we collected almost $10,000 dollars and with the government program now had

$20,000 of aid for Father Joe and his needs. In today's terms that would be around $80,000 to $100,000 and we know Father Joe put it to good use for the villagers in Swaziland.

I was initially disappointed that we had only reached $10,000 until the other workers got it into my head that 10,000 people had just given a dollar they would never miss, with no receipt being given, and around the world there were children who were learning how to grow their own food, were drinking clean water and had a community schoolhouse under construction.

The following year it was time to do it again but I felt the focus was shifting as others had joined with slightly different ideas, unnecessary expenses were being incurred, such as they wanted to use funds to fly me to meet the King of Swaziland etc, and in so many ways we were becoming just like all the other multitude of aid organizations, so I quietly stepped away and left them to it.

The message I leave you with here is the proof that any one of us can indeed make a difference and we do the moment we commit to it, and the ripple effects of your actions may never be fully made clear to you but you can rest easy in the knowledge that, at least for a moment you truly did Pay It Forward. Journey Well.

TWENTY TWO

*"All the King's horses and all the King's men.
Couldn't put Humpty together again."*

"All the King's Horses and all the King's Men, couldn't put Humpty together again." There is an addendum to that nursery rhyme that has been erased from our consciousness. "But Humpty never knew he could rebuild himself!" This is a story of how a man searched the world for the best King's horses and Men to help him and was truly giving up hope until he found the answer in the one place he hadn't looked. Inside his own heart.

T.J. is a retired businessman and extremely successful from a financial perspective. He lived in the perfect home, in the perfect location, surrounded by loving wife, children and grandchildren, in a most impressive residence, with stunning views all around. He and his family would never be financially insecure. There was nothing material that he had or could not obtain if he required. It should have been the happiest time of his life. Yet he did not have the one thing he needed most. His health.

Since retiring, T.J. had gradually lost the power in his arms and legs and also in a gradual process, the sight in his one good eye and was now quite depressed, almost bedridden and totally blind. His family despaired as they watched him deteriorate steadily.

He was truly a broken man and had indeed called in all the King's horses and all the King's men but to no avail. He had attended the top clinics on the planet, consulted with teams of specialists and still had no diagnosis. They even gave him his own disease. They named it the

T.J. Syndrome! They should have at least given him a T shirt with that on it, don't you think?

So, at the end of their rope, in desperation, his wife called me and asked me to come down to their paradise to see T.J. and so, a few weeks later my partner Jane and I were in their home deep in a part of the world I would never have been privileged to otherwise, and I began to work with T.J.

Within a few days we had him vastly improved from the perspective of his depression and functionally he was able to assist us more when we had to sit him up or transfer him to his wheelchair. This was slow but definite improvement, yet there had to be more.

We developed a good friendship quickly in the first few days and I felt ready to try to get him to the next level.

T.J. was still deeply angry at his former partners in business whom he felt had managed to take over his shares at far below market value (although remember he was still a very wealthy man at the end of it all). One day, sitting beside T.J. in his reclining chair/bed we moved the conversation gently forward. I began by asking him how he felt when his partners had behaved in the manner he perceived them to have behaved? He thought on this for a long moment, then he said one word "Betrayed." His wife glanced up from the book she was quietly reading on hearing him say this. He had never spoken of it before.

I paused for a moment then stated that I suspected that the feeling of betrayal was not a new experience. He agreed. So I asked him if, in fact, it was an all too familiar experience in his life, and again he agreed that this was indeed the case. I paused again then I asked him if he remembered the first time that he felt betrayed? He nodded silently. I asked if he could tell me who produced that feeling of being betrayed in him for the very first time? After a moment's silence he said "My Father."

So, there it was; the primal wound; the initial feeling of betrayal exposed at last. Always there, always trying to come to the surface for healing and therefore presenting itself in various forms, ever increasing until dealt with. So, in reality, the partners who had "betrayed" him were not an issue. Their actions were only created to bring something up in T.J. that needed to be addressed. Once admitted it began to resolve, it was that simple. Within 2 days T.J. had recovered his sight and was doing his own banking on the Internet again. Within a week he hosted his first dinner party in years at which we were included as grateful guests. He proved an interesting and skilful host to all present and happiness had returned to his home. He was able to sit up in a wheelchair for hours at a time and interact with family, friends and pets.

We left a week later happy to see the changes in T.J. and the relief in his children and grandchildren. Unfortunately I don't think T.J. progressed much beyond that point. He went into denial after we left, saying that it was simply his new lenses on his glasses which had restored his vision, although the timing didn't actually coincide at all. The glasses in no way could be attributed to the return of his physical functions and his increased mental alacrity, which returned before he got his glasses. Sadly his depression and apparent death wish returned and the last I heard was T.J. was deteriorating once again.

He had indeed found the moment when the path of his life changed and he had made a conscious decision just to accept the betrayals of life and move on. His life had manifested according to his mindset and even having found it was still torn by anger and grief and could not take the step of truly forgiving himself and releasing his pivotal decision, made when still an innocent.

He also was confusing Prosperity with Abundance! These are not the same thing!

Abundance is defined as "an overflowing fullness, great plenty, wealth . . . strictly applicable to quantity only" . . . while Prosperity is defined as "often encompassing wealth, but also includes other factors which are independent of wealth to varying degrees, such as happiness and health!"

So you can see that T.J. by definition indeed had manifested abundance but was a pauper from a prosperity perspective!

So even here the ties that bind surface . . . many sources get you to pray for or strive to manifest Abundance which in itself seldom brings happiness, when, in reality, by definition, you should have been manifesting Prosperity! . . .

To conclude then, firstly change your thoughts from abundance to prosperity and secondly, if you have negative feelings of betrayal, abandonment or unworthiness that keep manifesting as did T.J's, learn from him and find and release the source as he did.

I thank T.J. for the lessons he has now brought forth for all of us by courageously displaying his chosen path.

TWENTY THREE

Heroism is Not Spontaneous!

Heroism does not mean spontaneity! There have been several events in my life which have been deemed by some as heroic. I truly beg to differ. I believe with all my heart that there are certain times on our lives when, not by chance, we are placed to be of service to another. I believe that we have been placed synchronistically, and that we have suddenly appeared, almost like angels, to briefly interact with another in trouble. We simply do what needs to be done without thinking. Take a moment now to remember when such spontaneous angels, usually strangers, appeared in your life, and also when you have been a spontaneous angel to another.

A real hero is the one who weighs the risks, understands what it might cost them and still goes ahead anyway, like the firemen who put it all on the line knowingly and willingly, often every day, each time they enter a burning building to save another they are fully aware of the personal risk. Therefore there is a real difference between natural, instinctive compassionate spontaneity and true heroism. Everyone of us is capable of performing compassionate acts. I am not as certain that I possess the fortitude of heroism. I tell these stories now that you may firstly just enjoy them and then celebrate that these acts of love are happening everywhere, every hour globally, then open your heart to allowing yourself to being a very real part of it. Remember yourself as the angelic being you truly are.

While driving along the sun baked highway which slices through the rolling jet black lava fields on the west coast of Big Island, Hawaii, we were flagged down by another motorist warning us of an accident ahead. We drove cautiously on and pulled over before the actual accident scene and walked forward to assess the situation. There was a vehicle somehow balanced up on the jagged lava by the roadside. It was facing downhill, all windows and windshield were smashed and gone, the front and the rear of the car was like an accordion, yet the driver still sat in his seat, bleeding from a head wound and burned by the exploding airbag, but otherwise seemed alert and in no pain. We never did figure just how his vehicle ended up in this state or so precariously balanced. Several other motorists stood around his vehicle unsure what to do next. My partner, Jane, jumped back into our vehicle and drove about 80 meters beyond the crash site, laying out emergency cones that we always carried and began to slow and direct traffic coming from the north end of the island. There was a young lady already there who had been jumping into the middle of the highway to slow fast approaching vehicles, and she was very relieved to accept this structured assistance from Jane. Emergency services had been contacted and the medics and police were on their way, as was the trauma helicopter to evacuate the driver over to Oahu. The bottom line was this. The driver was struggling to stay calm, and reaching out his hand to connect with us. One man said he would like to help him but as there was blood on his (the victim's) hands he, and the others wouldn't touch him! That triggered me and I just stepped up and reached in to grab his hand for around ten minutes until the medics arrived. The relief to this terrified man because of this simple action was obvious. At one point I told him he was a brave man. He squeezed my hand a little harder, smiled weakly and said "Yeah, so far."

It was only later that we thought about how unstable the car had been balanced there. The fire crews and medics would not attempt to stabilize and remove him until they had braced up all of the wheels. If I had thought of it sooner I wonder if I still would have stepped up.

I know that many of you would have responded in the same way I did. No heroism just compassion. He didn't need all the king's horses in the moment we met. He simply needed someone to hold his hand!

But my "work" wasn't over! As the professionals stepped up to the vehicle I released my hand, wishing the trapped man good luck and stepping back down onto the highway. As I crossed the highway, another vehicle screeched to a stop and a young distraught woman jumped from it. She immediately seemed to freeze and could barely take a breath. It was the accident victim's sister. I was able to calm her somewhat by placing my hand on her heart and verbally reinforcing that her brother was ok, and that to see her upset would not be in his best interest. She bravely and quickly grounded herself again and was able to smile to him and wave supportively and confidently as the emergency crews began to cut their way into the vehicle. It was good to see him smile in return. I walked along the Highway towards our vehicle and told Jane and the young lady with her that all appeared to be well.

The young woman began to cry with relief, stating that was a good thing as now she had to continue to her brother's home and help his family as they had just been informed of his death a few hours previously! She was visibly shaking and I simply put my hands on her shoulders, looked her deeply into her eyes and said "So that will be twice today you have been asked to be an angel of support. What a beautiful gift you have brought to the world today. Thank You." We could see and feel the peace of this truth flood through her and her strength and indeed her light returned. She, for the first time began to understand her role that day and embraced it wholly. I am certain that she was indeed an angel of compassion for her family throughout their tragedy as she had been for others as she stopped, without thinking, to help a stranger in distress.

Next, the story of a exceptionally fit young man in real difficulty in the riptides and surf off the coast of Maui. My partner and I were enjoying somewhat turbulent waist deep water when I first heard his strangled cry and could see the terror in his eyes even from a distance. He had gone into much deeper water to get a plastic football that his buddies had thrown, which had overshot the intended receiver and landed in the fairly high surf just a little farther offshore. The biggest kid in the group went after it even although it was fairly rapidly being pulled away from shore. He soon realized that he wasn't going to catch up to it and then as he turned back was horrified to know that he didn't have any strength left to fight the current. His high pitched distress sounds were met with derision by his colleagues who thought he was jesting. Time really was of the essence. There were no lifeguards on duty at that particular beach.

Without thinking, I swam out to him and as I neared him then I suddenly realized that I couldn't grab hold of him as he was one very panicked adrenaline driven, muscular kid and could easily have pulled me down with him if I let him latch on to me. So I firmly and loudly told him to look me in the eyes, not at the shore. After telling him a couple of times, he did as I asked and visibly began to calm down. Next I heard myself tell him that we were going to make it to shore together; that he would do it on his own power and that we would do it one stroke at a time. His eyes were a little calmer now and he nodded in agreement. I swam sidestroke beside him, holding eye contact at all times and one stroke at a time we steadily advanced towards the shore until I told him he could probably touch bottom if he put his feet down. He did and with a last burst of energy wade to shore unassisted and collapsed in front of his laughing friends.

This time all that had been needed was sustained eye contact to give a man the strength to do what had to be done.

I didn't follow him onto shore but returned to my partner to allay her fears and assure her that I was ok.

Once again I had been placed in the right place at the right time and had acted without thinking, out of compassion for another, nothing more.

Once again it was only some hours later that the potential risks to myself were probably multiple and I again doubt that, if I had taken (or been given) time to think I would have responded to the situation as I did.

It was only later that the potential danger I had put myself in began to sink in to our consciousness and, again, I don't think I would have been so "compassionate" if I stopped to think about it first.

Further to that, I know that normally I would have been unable to swim as far as I did and back against the current. I had been a strong swimmer in my youth but that was a very long time ago and a few leisurely strokes were now my contented maximum. For a few minutes I completely forgot that I was a most unfit sixty five year old male.

Mr. Boom Boom! . . . now this one has a real funny ending and demonstrates how people confuse compassionate and intervention with heroism. We were in Buenos Aires Airport, returning to Canada. It was only a few days after the massive earthquake in Chile. We had been caught in it also as we had been in Bariloche, very close to the Chilean border and we had experienced a 6.9 earthquake which they said lasted for two and a half minutes, which, trust me, feels like an eternity.

Anyway, all was now well and we were returning home. Santiago airport was still closed due to the earthquake damage so Buenos Aires was trying to handle the flow of all traffic through its airport with great patience and much compassion for the unavoidable chaos created in the over full terminal. There was one restaurant with seating for around two hundred people, and my eyes were drawn to the only empty two seater table there, which seemed to light up to get my attention and we finally managed to struggle through and claim it as our own. I remember that feeling of the lone table 'lighting up' to get my attention and I firmly believe we were being directed to exactly the spot we would need to be to deal with upcoming events. We had three hours to kill so we were simply grateful and believed this would be a good spot to await our flight out. There was a good menu and I was sat facing my partner, and behind her high on the wall was a large TV showing soccer, which I enjoy, so I figured we were all set. How wrong I was! I glanced around and noticed several different scenarios without giving them much thought.

There was a man sitting below the television I was watching, two rows of tables in front of me. He seemed to have had a little too much to drink. Next to him were a beautiful family consisting of Mum, Dad, twin girls around twelve years old and a delightful, very cheerful three year old son. Next to me on my right were an elderly couple, each engrossed in reading, and next to them was a distinguished looking elderly gentleman, impeccably dressed and well groomed. He was alone and like me seemed to be enjoying the game on TV. I returned to some casual conversation with my partner. We were barely able to hear each other due to the interactions in Spanish going on throughout the restaurant, and, as we don't speak Spanish it all somehow added to the sense of adventure which was the way we lived our lives. Little did we know that the adventure was about to pick up the pace.

I first had just a sense that something wasn't right with the scene before me and found myself scanning the people around me again. On taking a slower and more lingering look I noticed that the man whom I thought was suffering from overindulgence of alcohol was beginning to perspire and was clearly now muttering to himself. The young family next to him were aware of his demeanor and were beginning to try to pull their chairs a little farther away from him. I glanced at the distinguished elderly gentleman to my right and he definitely seemed perturbed and was looking anywhere except towards the television set on the wall. Looking back at the increasingly agitated man seated under the wall television I saw that whatever he was muttering he was directing it at the now clearly unsettled elderly gentleman to my right. More than that he seemed to be gradually inching his chair to the left, which, when it cleared the confines of his table would give him a direct route to get at the elderly man! There was no time to think, no time to explain, I quickly stood and walked over to the elderly gentleman's table and sat down across from him, so that I was now between him and his potential attacker. I guess I hoped that this would be a deterrent.

The elder gentleman showed intense relief, greeting me warmly in English, although clearly Spanish was his normal language, as I joined him. We began a brief conversation. He asked where I was from and I told him Calgary. He relaxed even more and laughingly told me he liked Calgarians as he had played on line poker against them many times! Then he suddenly became somber again, saying "Senor, the man is staring at you." I sighed and said that I understood, still hoping that my presence would be sufficient to prevent escalation. I was wrong.

Suddenly, my new friend's eyes widened in fear, and it seemed as many people started screaming and I knew that the man seated under the TV was running at me and was only a few feet away.

I stood up and turned around, all in one movement, my chair flying off to the side. As I was turning I extended my right arm, locking my elbow and clenching my fist. The aggressive man ran straight into it, striking him over the heart area. He staggered back a few feet, then charged forward again, running straight into my clenched fist again. It seemed that everyone in the airport was yelling and screaming as the crazed eyed, profusely sweating individual ran into my fist for the third time.

"He killed my son!" he screamed.

"You're not getting near him," I replied.

He stopped for a second, staring at me then yelled "Then I kill you!" and ran full tilt into my fist again.

My partner was trying to get someone to call security in all the chaos, but even though this had been done it still took over almost five minutes for them to appear. During this time the pantomime continued of this clearly imbalanced individual running into my fist! I thought of ending it quickly with a punch to his head but I could see the family who had been beside him now clearly terrified and huddled together directly behind him and he would have landed amongst them so I rejected that thought. Then I remembered that we were in South America; security were on the way; and I got a mental picture of them arriving and arresting us both into custody without stopping to ask questions; so I hurriedly dropped any option other than purely defensive. I honestly was starting to tire a little and couldn't quite understand why no one had stepped in to help me, when security suddenly swept in. They quickly overcame my adversary and almost immediately he was taken away. They never talked to me or even looked at me! It was all over as quickly as it started.

I asked the gentleman whom I had "protected" if he was OK and he nodded in relief. I then walked over to the young family and chatted and laughed with the three children until they began to laugh with me and I could see they were really OK again. Their father shook my hand in gratitude before they left. I was then finally able to hug my partner and sit down again to discuss it with her. A short time later the elderly gentleman who had been the target of such anger came over to express his thanks before boarding his flight. He said he had no idea who the crazy man was but was just happy to be protected as he had been downright scared. I told him it was no big deal and told him to pay it forward someday, someplace. He agreed and again after expressing his gratitude, left, to fly safely home.

It was on our flight home that we realized that I may have been at risk, that the maniac could have easily been holding a weapon. Same old story of acting first, thinking later.

BUT IT DOESN'T END THERE!

Less than a year later we were returning from Argentina yet again! I had been invited back to help individuals and to teach a class. So here we were, sitting in the same airport restaurant in Buenos Aires awaiting our flight to Houston Texas. The restaurant was less than half full this time, there was peaceful music playing over the P.A. System and we were laughing and joking a little as we recalled how surreal our last time there had been.

Ready to leave, we walked over to the counter to settle up our account. The young supervisor suddenly pointed at me and started yelling, and I do mean yelling excitedly in Spanish! I (we) had no idea what was happening as waiters and waitresses came running tall, broad shouldered youth whom I remembered being there on the day of my altercation.

He was telling everyone within earshot "It is him . . . It is Mister Boom - Boom!" pointing at me.

He then described how every time this maniac ran at me I hit him with a left, then a right, then another left . . . "Boom, Boom, Boom," and I realized that there was an urban legend forming here, getting more bizarre every time it was told. Everyone was cheering and applauding!

"Let's get out of here now" I muttered to my partner. She grinned, telling me that she had never seen me blush before but I sure was blushing in that moment. We waved to the staff briefly saying Adios and beat a hasty retreat.

Once again I had simply been placed in the right place at the right time and had done exactly what I was supposed to, nothing more. As the story grows I'm sure the severity of the situation will also be exaggerated and grow accordingly and Mr. Boom - Boom will become the stuff of international legends!

So, if, in years to come you should pass through Buenos Aires Airport and you should see a statue to "Mister Boom - Boom" you will smile and understand just how deeply we crave heroes and how often we create them out of nothing, like magic!

I may never live down that name however as my partner coyly reminds me from time to time.

I honor each and every one of you for the unsung acts of spontaneity which you have performed in your lifetime and I acknowledge this form of heroism in you all, and hope you can permit yourself to accept my gratitude and that you will always honor this part of you that has touched so many more lives than you will ever know.

TWENTY FOUR

Building Bridges TO the Children

I have now related many true stories of my blessed interactions with gifted children and young adults globally. They are all too often labeled A.D.D., A.D.H.D., O.C.D., Non Verbal, Autistic, Asperger, Hyperactive, and multiple other labels signifying that they just don't fit into our model of society. Many compassionate people strive to build bridges FOR the children to cross over to us. I believe, and have tried to show repeatedly in this book, that the children are NOT the problem. They have brought the solutions to a world in chaos. We need to build our bridges TO them. They are just fine the way they are. In their simplest form they can be seen as evolution of the species. Other names such as Indigo, Crystal and Rainbow Children are also put upon them. These are well meaning, however, giving any child a label tends to indicate they are different or special. The whole point of these kids is that they are trying to show us that they are indeed the norm and that all the gifts they possess are just as easily accessible to each of us, if only we had as much faith as a grain of sand in the Law of Creation. Medicating and suppressing them is not the answer. Here are some other young adults that I have encountered and how they have dealt with life up to now.

Leilani, not her true name, is yet another for these "magical" ones. She lives in California now, but was raised on the magical Big Island of Hawaii by a most understanding mother. Leilani is a natural beauty of a woman, who simply manifests everything she needs! She thinks what it would feel like to own a pink laptop for example, and, within days she has been gifted one! She always wanted a red mini cooper car with white racing stripes when she was a child. Guess what she drives today? and it cost her very little! She lived in Hawaii, close to the water she loved and had a tall strong and handsome young boyfriend, everything she desires simply flows to her. When she was only three years old she was able to physically bend spoons from across the room. She thought this was normal and that anyone could do this but soon realized that it just made people think she was different or even thinking of her as a witch, so she stopped developing her gift of being able to alter her apparent reality. Please note that it is indeed an innate ability in us all. I learned this thanks to working with James Twyman, and have incorporated spoon bending into my classes with consistently amazingly and often hilarious results! But I am digressing. Back to Leilani.

One warm Hawaiian night, Leilani and her friends were on a deserted beach enjoying each other's company and the light from their crackling campfire. This was a favorite gathering spot for the local youths and indeed some of them (although only a small percentage) did indulge from time to time in marijuana and others in LSD. Leilani was not one of those, although she talks of how much she enjoyed being around the ones who had taken LSD!

She says that she has two ways of talking. One is in her everyday world where she has learned what is deemed to be proper conversation. The other is all about the universe and quantum physics which she simply understands, although never taught it. Leilani says that when some of the other kids were on LSD they actually understood the theories she put forward and she felt relaxed around them!

However, on this particular night there was potential trouble developing in the form of a local policeman on patrol on the beach on a motorized quad bike. He sped towards the kids and pulled up sharply, emerging from his self created cloud of sand to march purposefully towards the youths gathered there. He was well known to the youths and had a reputation of being heavy handed in his dealings with them on previous occasions.

He headed straight towards Leilani, eyes focused on her alone. She clearly remembers seeing the energy of light deep within him and thinking "We are all one" . . . "We are all one" as she knew that if he grabbed hold of her there would be an immediate protective response from the young men around her; and that this would give the officer the exact scenario he was looking for.

The patrolman got closer and closer until, within touching distance of Leilani he began to extend his arm towards her, then suddenly stopped as though frozen solid! His eyes seemed to soften and his exact words were "You know, at times like this I know that God puts angels on this earth!" he lowered his arm, stared at Leilani for a moment, then turned and returned to his vehicle and drove off into the night.

Leilani had simply projected pure love (as is her norm) and had by the law of creation, instantly resolved the scenario unfolding around her.

What amazing gifts these young ones bring. The biggest gift of all is their gift to us that we can discover the same gifts within ourselves.

Other kids, like Leilani, use their gifts to their advantage in life as simple professional life skills.

We met a beautiful young Canadian lady in Mexico, who told us that she was able to "read" men's thoughts ever since she could remember. It is impossible for them to lie to her or manipulate her on any level. She is making a VERY good living as a professional poker player! Another young lady with the same capability has a very successful track record working for C.S.I.

Unfortunately, refusing to bury their gifts does not always have a happy ending. I had an assistant school principal, let's call him Frank, seeing me for treatment to a sports injury and, in general discussion he told me of the dilemma he faced in school. He said that there often were times when young men of 15 or 16 years of age were sent to his office for punishment as they had told one of his teachers that he was full of crap! Frank's "problem" was that inwardly he agreed with them! However, it was his role to punish the boys for their behavior and he did so with a somewhat heavy heart. He talked of how these kids would go home from school, living in a socially deprived environment, and sooner or later their father's would come at them and how they would then tell their father's that they too were full of crap! The father/son conflict would clearly escalate by this stance and the kid would usually simply stay out of the home as much as possible. They would then hang out with other kids who felt the same and could easily be then construed as a street gang. Sooner or later some over exuberant law officer would challenge them and he would quickly be told that he had the same problem as their fathers and their teacher! So they get arrested, and now face a criminal record with all of its ramifications in life. Yet some people still wonder why they are angry? They are all about integrity. They will never tell a lie, no matter the cost. They have a built in bullshit detector for everyone they meet. They are the only ones in the whole scenario who have told the truth, yet they are the only ones being put down and punished. Of course they are raging. Wouldn't you?

These kids have their gifts but no one has taught them how to use them properly. Their anger (often created in their home environment) is the catalyst creating the scenarios in their lives which will emphasize how ultimately wrong they are to use their integrity until they surrender it altogether or become immersed in a world of criminals. If only they could be taught by their peers like Leilani how to maintain their integrity yet project their energy differently, the situations with teachers, parents and police would never have occurred. This is why building bridges TO them, where they can meet and exchange their gifts and the problems inherent with them, like we did in Bariloche, should be a priority for us all. How many of you can relate to these boys, how many of you can see the same issues developing in children around you? Can we now consider application of the Law of Creation and help them to understand it also?

TWENTY FIVE

The Law of Creation

In Mexico, some years ago, I truly learned the Law of Creation and how a stunningly simple formula taught by a mentor from the United States, showed me that my resistance was the only roadblock. I had just completed teaching my first workshop in Puerto Vallarta, Mexico. I was in deep gratitude that all had gone so well. The love and support I had been shown on every level had been almost overwhelming at times and beyond my wildest expectations. It was time now to prepare for my return to Canada in a couple of days. In my quiet time in Vallarta I relaxed by the hotel pool and had found myself reading the craft of a lady by the name of Elyse Hope-Killoran who had a website www.choosingprosperity.com. Her practical approach to creating prosperity of any kind just seemed to make sense to me, unlike many other "gurus" I had looked over from time to time. I still prescribe to Elyse's work on occasion to this day and recommend it for any of you to check out and decide for yourself. Anyway the part that was getting my attention in that particular moment was her simple formula for life which is "Manifestation = Desire minus Resistance." She claimed that to manifest or create anything in one's life you had to figure out how bad you wanted it (on a scale of one to ten) then realize how high your resistance was to actually believing it could happen (again on a scale of one to ten); then subtract your resistance from your desire and you had the true strength of your prayer. Seemed feasible to me so I thought, somewhat cynically, I'd put it to the test. So I thought about something I genuinely would like, and the first thing to pop into my head was how good it would feel to fly back to Calgary in first class seating on both of my scheduled flights. I am almost 2 meters tall and over 100 kilos in weight, so travelling in "coach" class presented several unpleasant challenges. So, I mused, this first class travel home is what I want to manifest? So be it. How badly do I want it? An immediate TEN sprang into my mind. So, next then, how high was my belief that it couldn't happen? Probably a three or a four was the answer there. So, in reality my wish was a ten minus four, making it only a six! The next little while was quite difficult as I argued with myself as to why I would resist? I really wanted it, no doubt in my mind, and realized that my resistance was actually stupid, so finally was able to drop it all and simply let my prayer sit as a ten. I honestly laughed to myself at this point and dove into the pool to cool off—promptly forgetting about the whole thing. Two days later I am at the Airport in Vallarta, surrounded by my wonderful Mexican friends who had all come to say "Vaya Con Dios" to me, as is their way. There was a long line up at check in and we moved very slowly forward, although enjoying good conversation along the way. My friend, Dr. Martina suddenly told me to take my bags over to the first class check in to sidestep the lineup as one of her patients was the clerk in that line and he had said it was OK. Feeling gratitude I stepped up to him, where he checked in my bags and then handed me two new tickets for my flights. I had been upgraded to first class! Whether the seats were still available or whether Dr. Martina had purchased the upgrades I never discovered, but I had told no one of my "experiment in manifestation."

As I sat in comfort in my front row first class seat awaiting take off for Phoenix I realized that this simple formula had just been proven, quickly and indisputably. I have used it many times since and it has always been a perfect monitor of my confidence in every situation. I had never thought of my desire again from the time I decided it was a ten until it actually manifested. A good friend helped me understand that when she told me "When you order a meal in a restaurant, you don't keep running into the kitchen every two minutes to make sure they are preparing it do you? Then it is the same with manifesting. You are clear on what you want, place your order and forget about it, confident that it will show up on your table exactly as you desired."

My incredible mother, then aged 84, could converse about any topic under the sun and did so enthusiastically to her family and many friends. A highly intelligent, life loving individual, I enjoyed challenging her perceptions from time to time. She called me once saying she had injured her leg when she had fallen from the counter top in her kitchen! (she had been washing her windows) I asked her what the heck she was doing standing up on the kitchen sink? Without a moment's hesitation she replied "Tap Dancing!" . . . enough said.

Raised in a strong Irish Catholic environment she had certain ingrained beliefs which I would tease her about when appropriate. One of those beliefs was that it is easier for a rich man to enter the kingdom of heaven than for a camel to pass through the eye of a needle (that may not be the exact wording but you get my drift). However, while she maintained her stance that poverty was the way to Paradise, she frequently complained about how expensive life was for her!

So, I asked her that while I wouldn't get into the rich guy/camel thing, didn't she ever pray for money? I was more than a little shocked when she firmly asserted that she prayed for money every single day! She even had a specific amount £2,000,000! Her intention was to use the windfall as an inheritance for her sons and grandsons. I definitely went along with that idea! So, I asked her on a scale of one to ten, how badly did she want the money? After serious deliberation she said it was probably a two!! Trying not to smile I asked her on a scale of one to ten what was her thoughts that it probably wouldn't happen? Again she focused then said it was probably around an eight! Therefore I was able to show her that her prayer was sitting at a vibration of negative six! This really got her attention and we discussed how she could lower her resistance and she has genuinely tried to be more open to this formula since. Well she doesn't have the two million yet, however she has seen her net worth rise steadily as money from unexpected sources keeps coming in, so seems as though her prayer has at least passed into a positive number. I had another patient, who in general conversation complained that nothing was happening in her life. I asked how badly she wanted change, her answer was a six. I asked her how high was her resistance to change, her answer was a six! Six Minus Six Equals Zero . . . and what was happening in her life? Zero.

Just in case you still doubt this formula, I now offer you undeniable proof.

Some years back, having enjoyed the *What The Bleep Do We Know?* movie, we decided to attend a three day conference in Phoenix, Arizona, where all of the teachers from the movie would be speaking. It was a brilliant time and I learned a lot from the scientists assembled there. One evening during the course my partner and I were sitting outdoors on the patio restaurant, surrounded by fountains and palm trees, under the typically warm, star filled evening sky that embodies the perfect winter climate there. I said to my partner how much I would love to be working in this environment as opposed to the arctic winters back in Canada. We both imagined how incredible that would feel and enjoyed the rest of the evening. We had no business or personal contacts in that area whatsoever. Less than a month later we were contacted by someone who wanted me to come to Phoenix to treat her. She was offering for us to stay in a small casita by her private swimming pool on her property and had access to a large clinic where I could treat from and where she could send me many other patients. We gladly worked out the details and were soon back in Phoenix.

The clinic was in a beautiful setting and we were stopped in our tracks when we realized that it was only three blocks from the conference center where we attended the conference! So literally we had stated our intent, truly desiring it to manifest, had absolutely no resistance to it happening, and in less than three months it had manifested!

If that doesn't convince you, nothing will!

I recommend you try and apply this formula yourself, pick a wish, drop your resistance, create the feeling inside of how it will feel to achieve/obtain it, then simply recreate that feeling as often as you can. Game over. You can't lose!

TWENTY SIX

Native American Vision Quest

Alone in the Desert in Arizona, spending three days and two nights with no food and five liters of unusually warm drinking water, I was living out yet another boyhood fantasy. In a landscape of extreme heat and cold; Cactus; Rattlesnakes; Vultures; Scorpions; Tarantulas; Javelinas (wild boars) and even Mountain Lions, set in stunningly beautiful sunsets and sunrises, I was experiencing a little of the trials and wonders of the Native American Vision Quest. It is a quest undertaken at some point by us all. It is a search for answers as to who we really are and what our role in life truly is. "Hoka Hey"—it was a good day to die.

I had been living my childhood dreams of Cowboys and of Native American Indians for some time. I had been to, and loved, Texas, which indeed is larger than life in every way, but it was in Arizona where I truly felt connected. Being in a land where real life cowboys and ranchers walk the streets, where it is legal to carry a firearm in public; walking the canyons of the Apache; Hopi; and Navajo tribes, feeling their presence and coming to understand their history and their tragedies seemed important for me. I loved the Sedona area and felt intensely connected and free there in my over twenty trips to visit. I was incredibly happy to actually be in Flagstaff on the legendary Route 66 (and of course to drive to and experience Las Vegas in neighboring Nevada); fly in an old, bright red, open biplane over the ancient red rocks around Thunder Mountain; to see the Grand Canyon; to take a hot air balloon ride at sunrise over the desert; to sit in the old mining town of Jerome, high on Mingus mountain enjoying a cold beer while watching the stunning sun set behind the ancient plateau, home to the legendary prophetic Hopi Indians, and listening to wonderful old time rock from the earthy and real bands playing in the old Connor Hotel, surrounded by Harley Davidson motorcycles. There is still a sense of the pulse of the Old West everywhere here and it is indeed a place where boyhood fantasies can come true.

I had searched out and experienced several authentic Native American Sweat Lodges and understood just how different they could be each time. My respect grew steadily as I realized the deep spirituality of these people and their constant connection to their creator and to the land around them. I began to understand that the War Dances before battle that I had seen in the Hollywood versions of the Wild West as a child were a far cry indeed from their real and deeply spiritual purpose. In fact the only movie I saw in Scotland that had any bearing on reality was the tragic epic *Soldier Blue* in 1974.

Before a coming conflict, the Sioux would indeed dance around their campfires in prayer for many hours, but it was not a dance to build fanaticism and fervor. As they danced they reflected on their current lives and considered any personal conflicts they were experiencing. They then asked forgiveness from anyone they felt they had judged or wronged. When they finally felt at peace with everyone they said the words Hoka Hey (It is a good day to die).

This is not the cry of the fanatic, as we were shown in the cinema, it was a calm statement from men who knew they may not survive the coming conflict, but if they did not return, they could die knowing that they had made their peace with all whom they loved. Quite beautiful in actuality. I came to understand some of the spirituality of the Sundance ceremonies and the Vision Quest which they undertook ritually. So I decided to attempt the Vision Quest experience for myself. I talked to all of my Native American Contacts and was directed all over North America, but nothing quite worked out although I did learn much more and meet some truly incredible people on the journey. After all my searching it should be no surprise that I was led right back to Sedona, where it all began for me and there I met the man who would prepare me properly for my experience and ultimately drive me into the desert wilderness, leaving me there to let it all unfold.

Don't be misled, my journey was nowhere similar to the Native Americans. I knew for sure that while I may experience some discomfort on some levels, and that I would return to a good shower, clean clothes and a cold beer when it was over. Plus I was going out only for a fraction of what they would have considered to be the allotted time.

I had been preparing for days, spending time quietly in and around Sedona, allowing my mind to begin to settle into the lower gears of relaxation. The day before my quest I had hired a guide to drive me out into the desert in his jeep so I might familiarize myself with what may lay ahead for me. A strange thing happened that day which only came into perspective some weeks later back in Canada.

As we stood in the desert and my guide pointed out the various plants etc, a low flying raven swept past us and landed in the branches of a small tree nearby, where it began to caw loudly and continually. My guide laughed saying that Raven welcomed me to the desert. For my part I thought that it must be a trained bird he brings out for tourists, but thought it was cool never the less! As we watched, the extremely loud Raven continue his raucous welcome, there was a blur across my vision as a hawk screeched just past my head at high speed and slammed into the raven, knocking him from his perch! Now that really is a good trick I thought. This guy has two pet birds and sets this act up for people like me. Brilliant! Well worth the money! He told me how that was really strange; how he had never actually seen that before; how the hawk could easily have sunk her claws into the raven and how the raven was more than capable of fighting back but had not done so as they were both winging their way almost together out into the distance. Again I put the whole thing down to part of the show and never gave it another thought.

Before taking me out to leave me, my guide had checked that I had all that I might need, and only that which I was allowed to take. He had taken me to meditate by the side of beautiful stream, held in respect by the local tribes; then up to a medicine wheel of stones and feathers where I again meditated and asked for support and guidance before embarking into the desert.

I watched my mentor's truck gradually disappear in receding clouds of dust and stood there gradually becoming aware of the feel of the steadily increasing blistering desert sun and of the all pervading stillness and absolute silence around me. My first chore was to decide where to lay out my waterproof groundsheet and sleeping bag, and where could I place my five liter plastic water bottle so it would be out of the sun's direct rays as much as possible. I put the water under one of the small scrub like juniper bushes that dot the landscape and finally selected a spot for my sleeping bag which was in an east west alignment and had magnificent views across the desert. I tried my best to stay out of the sun as much as possible that day by sliding myself under a juniper bush as far as I could and I decided to conserve as much energy as possible by simply moving only when I needed to. At one point I must have dozed off as I awoke with a start, opening my eyes only to see a vulture hanging motionless in the air, wings fully extended, less than two meters above me!

It thinks I'm dead I thought! I began yelling and scrambling out from under the bush as fast as I could, to prove that I was not ready to be devoured just yet. It must have been quite a funny sight to see. The vulture veered off to my right and I could hear his wings flapping slowly and rhythmically as he moved on in search of another source of protein!

I settled back into the late afternoon sun feeling relieved that night would soon fall and the heat would dissipate. Then I became distinctly uneasy as I realized that I would be far from alone in the night. It was in the cool nights that the rattlesnakes left their dens and the tarantula spiders and the scorpions also came out in search of food! I resolved to light a small fire to get me through the first part of the darkness, then further resolved to keep my sleeping bag tightly zipped around me and not to get out for toiletries until after sunrise.

Well firstly the silence and splendor of the desert sunset was a spectacularly colorful and deeply moving personal experience. My mind was actually beginning to slow down from its normal hectic chatter and I was actually beginning to enjoy myself, any pangs of hunger appeared to be eased by an occasional sip of water. My fire gradually became a pile of softly glowing embers and I lay in my sleeping bag absolutely mesmerized at the beauty and clarity of the millions of stars in the startlingly clear sky overhead. Occasionally I would track a high flying plane and wonder where it was headed, I could even spot and follow occasional satellites! Shooting stars seemed to flash across the sky in seconds and I saw at least ten of them throughout the magical night. I would often pinch myself to see if I was dreaming or was I actually living part of the magical life I had longed for as a child. I don't think I slept much, my only nervousness being when I simply HAD to leave the safety of my sleeping bag for toileting reasons and then realized that all things that crawl or slither in the night were definitely active and wondered if anything had slipped into my sleeping bag awaiting my return! I kept my jeans tucked inside my socks and my shoes stayed on as I returned from the chilly night air, but all was well and soon the dawn's light, preceding the sun's first rays began to brighten the horizon behind me.

The next morning passed uneventfully and it seemed very slowly as I began to feel more than just a little hungry but knew I had to use my water sparingly if it was going to last me for three full days. Many strange things happened during the rest of my time out there, but for this story I will only relate two. On the afternoon of the second day I was aware of light breeze which at first was welcomed indeed. However it seemed to pick up into a constant wind, along with the constant sounds of a blowing wind and I began to feel myself getting irritated at it! After all I was paying good money to be out here in the silence . . . and this wind was certainly not silence. My aggravation increased until I finally lost my composure and actually was yelling at the wind to shut up and actually punching the air around me in my frustration! Again this must have been a comical sight. Suddenly I realized that I was fighting the wind . . . and a small quiet voice inside me reminded me that I had been doing that my whole life (since I was ten years old actually)! In the second that I made this connection, the wind died down, the silence returned and I was left standing there again reflecting on my epiphany, tears streaming silently and unexpectedly down my cheeks.

It was around 2 a.m. the following morning quite hungry now, but unusually peaceful. I was sitting on top of my sleeping bag, again enjoying the wonders of the night sky when I became aware of a VERY loud purring close behind me. I instantly knew that I was hearing a mountain lion or cougar and that she was close indeed. I felt absolutely no fear as the sound I was hearing was not a growl, it was a purr, the kind a cat makes when it's contented, there was absolutely no threat in its energy whatsoever. I didn't want to turn around in case I spooked it in some way, so for around twenty minutes or so I simply embraced the incredible experience. I'm not sure when she left as I was simply aware that I could no longer hear her and I was somewhat saddened that she was gone, I settled down and had my first real sleep since I began my quest.

The following morning left me wondering if I had imagined or dreamed my visit from the big cat, however when I walked a short distance behind my sleeping bag she had left unmistakable paw prints in the desert floor to verify her presence.

The third day passed peacefully, even the hunger was tolerable as I finished the last of my water as I somewhat reluctantly watched my mentor's jeep create a distant dust cloud as it returned to take me back to civilization.

I did, however, thoroughly enjoy a long refreshing shower and then the sounds of people around me chatting as I sat in the shade on a patio restaurant enjoying a full lunch and a cold beer.

I was back in Canada a few days later and while shopping for groceries I was surprised to see that there was a community notice about a meeting to be held that evening for anyone who was interested in doing a vision quest! Intrigued I decided to show up and just observe what they were all about. I went along to the local community hall where there were around thirty individuals, clearly from many walks of life who had gathered for more information on the topic. The meeting was being run by a gentle natured lady who clearly understood the concepts of the Vision quest and was confidently fielding all questions put to her on the subject. She then gave several places in Canada where anyone could participate reasonably safely in this endeavor if they were drawn to do so. She then told us that she wanted to discuss the meaning of Power Animals or Totem Animals as they were known to the Native Americans. She said they often appeared on a quest and should always be given serious consideration for the gifts they bring us. I hadn't actually given this much thought and really didn't give it too much credence in that moment, until she suddenly stopped and asked if there was anyone in the room who had actually done a vision quest. I cautiously raised my hand. She asked me my date of birth and when I told her, she went to a large book she had in front of her and thumbed through it until she found what she was looking for. She seemed about to read what she had found, then stopped and turning the book face down on the desk she asked me to tell the audience the animals I had seen. I, of course recounted the vulture and the cougar plus the raven and the hawk prior.

She smiled as she turned the book over to reveal for all to see that my Indigenous Power Animals according to my date of birth, one for each of the four directions, were The Condor, The Raven, The Panther and The Red Tailed Hawk! Everyone sat there quite stunned, me most of all, before excited applause erupted around the room as the group leader exclaimed "I just LOVE when this happens."

I never did ask about the book she had, although many people I have met since are aware of it.

From that day on I gave a lot more gratitude to my experiences and paid a lot more attention to the lessons I had learned about myself out on the desert. I thanked my power animals for showing up, I believe simply to show me that I was being protected throughout my journey.

I can now discuss these totems as needed over the years and have found on occasion that many people are terrified of their "power animals" as they kept having dreams about them when they were children (which they thought were nightmares as the animal seemed to be constantly chasing them). I remember one young woman, around thirty years old, who, in discussion, happened to mention how she had always been terrified of polar bears. How, as a young girl they seemed to chase her relentlessly in her dreams until finally disappearing in her early teens (after she made her decision to disown her own truths and forcefully accept society's no doubt). She said that, as we chatted, she suddenly remembered a time when her parents took her to the Calgary Zoo for the day. She clearly recalled that she was 9 years old. She was in the polar bear and seal structure and there was a massive glass wall looking into the polar bear tank, so the public could view the bears swimming underwater.

She recalled standing on the little foot rail along that wall, one hand supporting herself against the glass, the other holding her little camera to her eye ready to take a snapshot should a bear appear. Suddenly the bear was looking at her face to face, its giant paw pressed against the glass exactly where her hand was! She screamed, taking a picture instinctively and almost fell as she jumped back as far as she could. She told me that the picture came out, and in fact she still had it, and the bear's paw seemed to be touching her hand and it did not look aggressive at all as it gazed deep into her eyes. I laughingly asked her what did her power animal have to do, shake her by the hand and smile for her camera before she would understand that it was not chasing her but simply staying close to protect her, if we are to believe the story of power animals? She cried tears of happiness and relief for some time as it all felt right and simply made sense to her now.

If only we would encourage our children to discuss their favorite or most feared animals, we may find we have much to learn.

TWENTY SEVEN

The Power of the Spoken Word

I was working in a wonderful treatment center, on a sunny, Saturday morning in St. Louis, Missouri. The patient I was about to see was special indeed. She was an eight year old child, we'll call her Chrissie as I do not want to reveal her real name or location. Chrissie had been traumatized by her biological father, whom we were told was currently in prison. Chrissie was in the protective custody of a foster family. She frequently complained of a stiff neck so her foster Mum brought her to me to see if I could help. Chrissie is a terrific kid with a great smile. She greeted me warmly and we chatted for a minute or two about how she liked school, what her favorite toys were etc, then I told her that I was going to try to help her get rid of her stiff neck. I told her that she would simply have to lie on her back on the treatment table and my hands would be supporting her head and working gently on the back of her neck. I also told her that she could say stop at any time if she needed to. She readily agreed and let me begin to work on her. I felt her relax almost immediately as I began working on her and I gently started to relax the muscles around her neck. Suddenly Chrissie said "Stop." I immediately relaxed my fingers and stayed still. She was quiet for around a minute, then she giggled and said "Go." I immediately resumed treatment, with a growing certainty that this could be a game between us unfolding. Sure enough, a minute or so later "Stop," quickly followed by "Go." The frequency of stop/go interspersed with loud giggling increased rapidly and her foster mother was now also laughing loudly, seated beside her. It was a lot of fun and

Chrissie was clearly enjoying being the ringmaster. Then, without warning, everything changed. Chrissie's tone changed completely as she suddenly screamed "STOP!" and jumped off of the treatment table, storming out of the room and almost taking the door off of the hinges as she slammed it behind her! Her foster mum was horrified and apologized profusely. I told her not to apologize but to go and be with Chrissie. I did not see or hear from them again that day. Three days later I heard from the foster mum, who called to say that Chrissie had been fine when she found her, and they had a good weekend together and that Chrissie hadn't mentioned her outburst again, so she thought all was well. However, on the Monday afternoon, while Chrissie was back at school, the foster mum had received a call from the school principal, asking if she would come and collect Chrissie! Never having received this kind of call before, the foster mother was quite startled and asked what was wrong, was Chrissie in trouble of some kind? The answer was "I'm afraid so!" Apparently Chrissie had been playing with a basketball at lunch time and an older boy had tried to take it from her. Chrissie told him to stop, but he persisted. She told him to stop again and yet again, and when he didn't, she had punched him on the side of the head, knocking him to the ground and effectively stopping him! I'm sure you now understand that when Chrissie said "Stop" to me on the Saturday it was the first time in her life that she had said the word stop to another human being and they actually did as requested. She had rediscovered the power of the word stop and was not going to relinquish that right under any circumstances. Her inner unicorn was well awakened now.

I thought that was the last I would hear from Chrissie. However, the following weekend I was teaching a workshop in a large College in St. Louis. We arrived early on the Saturday morning and parked at the end of a long car park. As I left my vehicle I heard my name being called. I turned around and saw Chrissie running towards me from the far end of the car park, where her foster mum's car was parked. She was just beaming as she ran at me and jumped up into my arms, giving me the biggest, longest and most wonderful hug I have ever received. Then she gave me a big kiss on my cheek, jumped down and ran back to her waiting foster mum. I never saw her or heard from her again.

So learn from Chrissie that Stop means Stop. Apply it to your own lives and feel how empowering it is. You don't have to justify why you are saying it. You just need to have your wish respected. Hopefully you don't have to punch anyone out to prove your sincerity!

TWENTY EIGHT

6.9 Earthquake

Experiencing and surviving a 6.9 earthquake was a most unsettling experience and was one which gives an acute awareness of our own mortality to anyone who experiences it. However, the realizations we experienced later seemed much more surreal.

It was 3:03 a.m. in Bariloche, Argentina. My partner and I were both jolted awake in our hotel room, as our minds struggled to grasp what was happening. My recollection was that the large painting on the right hand side was repeatedly slamming loudly against the wall about once every second. In my effort to make sense of it, my first thought went to the young couple in the room beyond that wall and I thought it must be their honeymoon! That thought quickly dissipated as I realized that it was the whole building that was rocking and therefore violently slamming the picture against the wall. The next awareness was of the cacophony of sound of what sounded like sirens filled the air also. We later realized that this was the sound of every car alarm in the area being triggered by the force of the ground movement. We scrambled out of bed trying to make sense of it all as we staggered around trying to sort it out. On reflection, I was pretty well useless, as three times I asked my partner what the heck was happening and three times she replied that it was an earthquake! I guess my mind just didn't want to hear that answer! So, I get myself half dressed and ready to go, while she has dressed and collected our passports, cash and bottled water to take with us! Yes she certainly is quite the lady. We stagger down the unlit and quite violently moving staircase and, along with other guests, we get outside and scattered. We found ourselves just a few feet away from the hotel, hanging on to the side of the outdoor hot tub, as the ground literally was heaving and rolling beneath our feet. There were another couple also hanging on grimly to the hot tub, she crying hysterically, he swearing loudly. The building beside us was creaking ominously as it still slammed from side to side. The small stream running through the property was sloshing water over its banks like an overfull bath tub on a storm tossed ship. There seemed to be a huge warmth coming through the ground also.

There is a complete respect for nature when you are caught in something of this magnitude.

You understand in an instant that the true power belongs only to her. You realize that this force is totally beyond our control and that nature is doing it quite effortlessly! If ever the phrase awe inspiring was appropriate in my life, it was in that moment of awareness. Then suddenly it all stopped and the stillness and silence returned around us (the car alarms had all stopped some time before although we hadn't noticed). In those moments I became clear that we are NOT killing the planet. She will survive our atrocities. The only question is whether we, as a species, will survive and learn to co-exist.

We sat down on a small retaining wall and tried to comprehend what had just happened. Thankfully it was a warm summer's night so the temperature was not a problem. The small hotel's manager showed up, a little shaken up [no pun intended]. He had got his internet working and it had shown him that close by, in Conception, Chile the epicenter of the earthquake had been an unbelievable 9.5 magnitude. It appeared to him that we had been hit with a 6.9. He told us that our quake had lasted 3½ minutes, which is unusually long, however, although time does appear to stand still in these scenarios, we know for sure that it lasted almost 15 minutes in total! My first thought was to get the word out that we were OK, so, maybe foolishly, I ran back inside the hotel and returned outside with my laptop. I was able to Skype my mother in Scotland and let her know that the news would be full of this disaster and that my partner and I were safe and completely unharmed. Now and again the plants and trees would begin to wave rhythmically from side to side as the aftershocks began rolling through, causing us a little apprehension. At one point a poor dog came timidly towards us, clearly terrified by it all and simply wanting to be around people, sat at our feet, trembling. Daylight came early and around 5 a.m. we actually returned to our room and rested on top of the bed, knowing that aftershocks could happen at any time. None of this makes sense now on reflection, but I swear to you this is how it all transpired.

I was supposed to be teaching a class the following morning and at eight-o-clock we were downstairs as agreed, and my students were actually beginning to arrive! The pots, pans, dishes, crystals that had been strewn around the floor had been cleaned up. The sun was shining and it appeared to be just another beautiful and pleasant morning. It was becoming more surreal by the minute. All of my 25 class members showed up on time and the first order of the day was obviously for everyone to describe their experiences of the night before. It was only then that I realized that it was a first time experience for them too! Many were simply too afraid to even get out of bed until it stopped. Others, like us had ran outside of their homes and fled as far from them as they could. We agreed to start the class and we carried on that day, although stopping apprehensively several times, as the hanging plants began to sway gently then settle down again as the aftershocks continued to roll through the area. It was only as the day progressed we all began to realize the stark and completely unfathomable truth that something was very abnormal about the whole event. We knew how prolonged and violent it all had been. Yet there were no reports of injuries to people, no damage to property, not even a broken window, no disruption of services or to power lines, roads, etc. and life had returned to normal as quickly as within a few hours! This made absolutely no sense on any level to any of us as I'm sure it baffles some of you as well. We then began to realize that, in our small hotel while dishes, ornaments etc. were strewn around, not one plate or dish was broken, yet they had littered the stone floor. It truly was miraculous and on so many levels makes absolutely no sense to us to this day.

However, we then began to recall a story told to us by our friends in Hawaii. A few years ago, The Big Island was hit by a 5.5 earthquake early one Sunday morning at around 7:30 a.m. The couple whose story I will now speak of are intelligent hardworking business owners, well respected throughout their community and not prone to exaggeration. I will call them Julie and Ed for confidentiality purposes. Apparently when the quake hit, there was no warning and dishes fell and paintings came crashing off of the walls in their home. Although Julie had never experienced an earthquake before she immediately grasped what was happening and for some reason went and stood in a doorway in their house. Somewhere in the recesses of her mind she remembered that this is what she should do, if such an unlikely event ever transpired. The quake seemed to increase in severity until Julie clearly remembers the feeling that her home, with her in it, was falling (dropping) straight down like an elevator as though the ground had opened up and swallowed them.

All she remembers is feeling anger that Ed wasn't there with her at that moment, as he was already out on the ocean piloting their charter boat.

Suddenly the feeling of falling stopped and all was still. She cautiously opened her eyes and found that her home was exactly as it should be, perfectly normal again and the sun was shining on a now peaceful again Sunday morning. All around Big Island damage reports were coming in of power lines being down, power outages, roads uplifted and shattered, buildings cracked, bridges collapsed. It was serious indeed. Yet as everything began to return to normal it was realized that there were zero casualties which made no sense at all given the circumstances.

Julie cannot explain her vivid experience other than this. She believes that the dimensions on the planet are crossing into each other frequently now. She believes that the evolutionary shifts promised for 2012 have been manifesting for some time now. She believes that on one dimension there would have been many casualties and on this one zero. Could the same thinking be applied to our night in Bariloche? I leave that for you to decide. I do know that miracles abound and have truly experienced one that night in far away Patagonia.

As a somewhat humorous side story, another friend, living on the other side of the Big Island, was in the shower when the quake hit and terrified raced through the house to her front door to get outside. As she opened the door she realized to her horror that she was naked and ran all the way back through the house for her dressing gown before leaving; proving that she would rather die in a natural disaster than run outside naked! Too funny.

TWENTY NINE

The Wheel Turns Full Cycle

Roslin Chapel, Dan Brown, Knights Templar, Holy Grail and all that stuff of myth and legend.

Or is it? I was about to find out! Have you ever just allowed your life to flow and found synchronicity to be your normal? It is something we should be doing all the time in actuality. However, perhaps this true tale of letting go will help inspire you to take the same approach to your life, if only for a short time.

I had just gone through my second divorce. It had been an extremely painful and harsh experience on every level for both parties.

I felt totally shattered and lost as to how to move ahead on any level. In fact I was probably considering whether I should stick around on the planet at all. A good friend once told me that sometimes you have to go back to your roots to figure out where you are headed. This seemed like my only option, so I flew back to Scotland, and after a brief visit with my parents, I decided to rent a car for three weeks and just drive around Scotland. I determined to have no planned route, just go wherever the road led me without worrying about the destination or the future. I was actually letting go and allowing my intuition to guide me although I didn't realize that at the time. I just wanted to ease the emotional turmoil. I guess that, on reflection, I was doing my own style of vision quest in my homeland. I believe that we are all connected to our homeland in far deeper ways than we have understood and that there is much healing for humanity by acknowledging that connection in each of us. Let me take you now to share my magical, mystical journey through the healing power of Scotland.

I found myself by the Bonnie Banks of Loch Lomond, the dark mysterious loch of ancient secrets, home to the Celtic Druids, and home to the unsung Kess (now called St. Kessog) the Celtic monk who came to Scotland 100 years before the legendary St. Columba came to Iona.

As I settled in to the energy there in the spot which I believe is one of the true secrets of Scotland, there were many times when I had to stop the car as tears literally blinded me. I found myself at the foot of Ben Ledi, another ancient druid gathering place and again so many tears flowed I wondered if it would stop, yet now, each time the tears ceased there was a feeling of peace beginning to flicker around my heart. I suddenly thought of Pluscarden Abbey in the Highlands, another spot surrounded by mystery and legends, and the Abbot's name was Hugh Gilbert! Seriously! [He has since moved on and is currently the Bishop of Aberdeen] So I thought I'd drive up there and meet myself, so to speak.

As I drove the long way there, through the Beautiful Trossachs area, I spent the night at Balquhidder, the home of the grave of Rob Roy Macgregor, the Scottish Robin Hood and I sat for some time in the magical fairy glen behind the grave. I felt at times that I could simply fade into the landscape here, a feeling I have never forgotten. As I turned North and moved up through Perthshire, past Stirling Castle, high on the volcanic plug dominating the plain around it, I genuinely became aware of the beauty that is Scotland. It seems that every single bend in the road blessed me with a view more stunning and spectacular than the one before and I was truly filled with awe and gratitude for the gifts being showered upon me. Stopping for lunch or for the night whenever I felt drawn to, everything was beginning to feel like a magical and easy flow, something I had longed for all my life. Each stop brought their own jewels to me and the tears still flowed suddenly and without warning yet were diminishing in frequency as I began to truly relish what may lie ahead. I reached Pluscarden and the deep energy of this place touched me immediately. I could feel it long before I arrived there. Even the monks there somehow seemed magical and Gandalf like to me. I strolled the grounds and the Abbey for hours before feeling it was simply time to move on (a feeling that would accelerate daily from this point on). Abbot Hugh was away at a conference and another monk laughingly told me that one of those

Hugh Gilbert's was quite enough at a time, thank you very much! I found myself grinning about this being "moved on" as I drove north again. It was at my next stop that everything began to shift and accelerate.

Culloden Moor, the site where a nation died, betrayed by their own kind and massacred by a vastly superior and better armed force, was my next stop. I had never been there before and didn't even realize it was on my itinerary. My heartache returned as I walked the massacre site (it should never be thought of as a battle) and I realize just what had been lost to Scotland on that day and forever since. I didn't realize how deeply I was connected to Scotland until this exact moment as I stood by the supposed mass graves of the clans at Culloden.

I walked into the bookstore as I left thinking maybe I should buy something to read when and as time presented. One book stood out, right at head height and I was drawn to it instantly. It was: *Rosslyn: Guardian of the Secrets of the Holy Grail* by Tim Wallace-Murphy and Marilyn Hopkins. This book had nothing to do with Culloden (that lesson was now over). I had no idea who or what Rosslyn was or for that matter The Holy Grail or the Knights Templar, so I didn't understand the strong impulse I had to purchase the book—immediately. Remembering my intent to go with the flow, I indeed did make the purchase and put the book in a paper bag on the passenger seat beside me and drove into Inverness to find accommodation for the night as the setting sun cast a sparkling light show on the waters of the Moray Firth.

I knew I was close to yet another mystical spot, the community of Findhorn, so I thought I'd make my way there and stay for a few days, soaking in the energetic of the place and maybe read the book I had purchased. Driving around the Findhorn area I could see why an environmentally aware community had grown there. It is a truly peaceful spot, complete with its own micro-climate allowing an abundant variety of crops to be grown. There are many historic healing wells scattered around the countryside in this area of Scotland, testimony to the wonder of this land. Happy to be there I began looking for lodgings and was a little unsettled as I realized there was absolutely nothing available due to a major environmental conference taking place there for the net six days! I was being "moved on" again and I set off meandering down the shores of Loch Ness and into Fort William, Oban, Mull and Iona. Swept away by the beauty and energy of these places I began to find some time in the evenings to begin reading my book. I was drawn to every facet of it and my curiosity only grew as I read it.

In every place I stayed in I could only get accommodation for one night and was therefore swept down the west coast until I arrived at a place called Kilmartin Valley.

Kilmartin Valley, the Valley of the Ghosts, held me in its grasp for a full day as I first walked the cemetery there, with so many Knight Templar graves together (a spot I had difficulty leaving) then walked in the ancient stone circles strewn around the area and the even more ancient graves, over 3,000 years old, and actually was able to climb inside one and meditate quietly as to where my life had gone and where it was going. I stayed in the historic and stunningly beautiful town of Inverary that night and in the morning had a strong impulse to call a friend in Glasgow. I had spoken to no one since setting out on my quest so this was a surprise to me, however I followed my instincts and made the call. After initial pleasantries I told her of my fascination with the book I was reading about Rosslyn Chapel. Her reaction startled and galvanized me into a decision that would shape the next few years of my life!

Loch Lomond, Christmas morning.

THIRTY

Doors Unlock, Mysteries Revealed, Others Take Their Place

Doors unlock, mysteries revealed, others take their place as my heart is given an energetic it had not experienced before. The magic and miracles of life continue to unfold.

The lady whom I called in Glasgow was clearly horrified by my reading material and my destination! She sounded quite upset, telling me with mild hysteria in her voice, not to go to Rosslyn Chapel, that nowhere else on earth were heaven and hell so close to the surface. I was stunned, as up to now I had thought of her as a rational, down to earth type of individual, not given to ghosts or goblin thinking in any way. She went on to explain that she had worked there for a time helping to clean and restore the intricate stonework and to help devise ways to remove the centuries of damp that had pervaded the structure. She said that there was such a deep sadness in the air there that she couldn't stay and could never return.

I thanked her profusely for her input and, having ended the call, I decided to point my vehicle straight at Rosslyn and not stop till I arrived there! I had to find out for myself what kind of place could produce this extreme response in a very practically attuned individual.

It was late evening when I pulled up in front of the two parallel hotels which the village offers to accommodate tourists. The first had a sign outside saying no vacancies so I went into the second one and asked if they had any availability. The receptionist almost apologetically told me that they were full also. I felt thoroughly exhausted and was about to thank her and drive on to Edinburgh when she suddenly asked me to wait, as there in fact was one room available! She seemed truly bewildered and said she had just checked the book ten minutes previously and it showed as full! I heard myself asking her that I didn't suppose I could get two nights? She laughingly said that was impossible, then as she flipped the page of reservations, once again seemed genuinely shocked that the same room was now available for tomorrow night too! I quickly secured the room for myself knowing that I was surely meant to be here, as it was the first time I hadn't been shunted on in my journey around Scotland. I slept soundly that night in a beautiful Victorian style room, unaware that I was sleeping only about a hundred meters from the beauty, the magic and the mystery that is Rosslyn Chapel.

As I enjoyed a full Scottish breakfast the following morning I remember feeling strangely calm and free of expectations. Finally ready I left the hotel and seeing the sign to Rosslyn Chapel I decided to walk there in the bright early morning sunlight. I hadn't quite realized that it had been at least three days since I had shed a tear of sorrow or self pity!

Soon I was standing outside the strange and intricately carved structure that is Rosslyn Chapel. It seemed quite small compared to my expectations and I entered through the open north door. This was about a year before Dan Brown's *The DaVinci Code* bulleted Rosslyn into the spotlight and renovations to accommodate the coming hundreds of thousands of visitors would be put in place. The Rosslyn Chapel I entered was very dimly lit and took a while for my eyes to adjust. It was also cold, the early morning late April sunlight unable to penetrate the thick damp walls. After walking around the inside of the chapel, completely intrigued by the thousands of intricate carvings covering the walls and the ceiling, I went down the staircase to the chamber beside the famous Apprentice Pillar. There is an altar at the far end which I was drawn to. I intuitively reached up to feel on the ledge at its head and found several large scallop seashells, some with handwritten notes in them! These proved to be from pilgrims who still walk the ancient Camino de Estrellas (The Way of The Stars) from Compostella in Spain, through France, ending at Roslyn! I determined to find out more of this clearly important point of Scotland and wondered why I had never been told of it in history in school. I then sat in one of the pews and quietly just settled in to the energy of the place. I had been completely alone in the chapel up to that point (an experience in itself that would be impossible to replicate today) and far from being afraid I realized that with every passing moment it felt like I had somehow returned home! I was filled with a deep sense of peace and decided simply to enjoy it without trying to figure it out. I was acutely aware of the Knights Templar connections to this so called chapel, from reading my book and somehow resonated with a strong sense of understanding to these connections, although I had never even given the Templars a moment's thought in all my life. That connected feeling was becoming stronger with every minute I sat in quiet contemplation in the Chapel. I didn't understand it then, and still really don't, but I simply accepted that this was what I felt in that moment. I have no idea of how long I sat there before I noticed that a young couple had entered and were walking slowly around the side aisle, enjoying the diverse architecture. I relaxed into my meditation again and a few minutes later was almost startled to find them standing in front of me, looking at me! I think I said Hi! and they both grinned and returned my greeting. The young woman waited a moment then said "You are one, aren't you?" Somewhat confused I asked her to explain what she meant. "A Templar Knight" she replied. "You definitely have been one in a past life and that's why you have returned here today," she continued, quite confident in the accuracy of her words. I told her that was a cool idea but I genuinely didn't know if I was or I wasn't and I honestly didn't give it much importance one way or another. Unperturbed she said "OK then, tell me how you came to be here today." I was warming to this young couple and truly had not had a lot of human conversation in the past two weeks, so I suggested that we go for coffee in the small cafeteria, and chat. It turns out that Nora was a movie producer and director of some acclaim and was researching Rosslyn with her colleague as part of a future project. The more I explained the series of synchronicities that had brought me there, the more they both just kept smiling at me until I realized that I had indeed been brought there intuitively but for what purpose I didn't know at that time. We parted some three hours later as friends and we still correspond occasionally to this day. I spent the rest of the day in and around the Chapel still grounded by that incredible feeling of having come home and its accompanying peace. After another perfect night's sleep I drove on back towards Glasgow knowing that my "vision quest" was at an end and I had indeed found what I was looking for.

I again reflected on how, as a young lad I had created a future full of travel, full of the Wild West, Cowboys, Indians, Rocky Mountains, Prairies, Deserts, plus Surfers and Hawaiians.

However, I couldn't recall any particular time when being a knight appealed to me, so it didn't really fit the pattern of my belief of how we create our own future.

Suddenly I remembered that I had in fact written the school play when I was only nine years old and it had been a tale of knights and maidens in distress etc. I had cast myself as a knight wearing a white robe with a red cross upon it. A Templar Knight! . . . now it appeared that even that short period of immersion was manifesting itself also, and indeed it most certainly proved to be the case in the following few years.

Perhaps you should take a few reflective minutes again now to remember ALL of your childhood dreams (potential creations) and have they come true? If not, can you identify when they have indeed tried to surface and how you managed to successfully sabotage them?

My next few years were spent investigating the History of The Knights Templar, including much personal involvement with their organizations and learning their amazing story. I have sat in conference with some of their most respected leaders whom I know and am proud to call my friends. There is such love and peace in Roslyn Chapel that is truly hidden in plain sight and it is indeed a beacon for a better world, which is not a New World Order to be feared. For those who wish to find out for themselves, just sit there for a while and meditate quietly on your life. [This was almost impossible to achieve after *The DaVinci Code* came out as the noise from visitors and guides was so loud and constant, and, I feel deliberately cheated!] As you sit there embracing the quiet energy you will realize the truth of the saying that you do not connect to Rosslyn, she will connect to you! Michael Bentine, a renowned British Comedian, suffered the heartrending loss of his children. He is quoted as saying that the only place in Britain where he felt he could connect to them was in the quiet of Roslyn Chapel.

Nothing in Roslyn was built or engraved as simply ornamental. Everything has a message and you will find more on every visit.

Yet there is only one written carving in all of the intricacies of Roslyn Chapel and it struck a deep chord within me. There was no fear of hell or Satan on this statement but I know it will strike fear into those who would control us. I will end this chapter with this truth and prophecy:

"Forte est Vinum; Fortior est Rex; Fortiores sunt Mulieres; Super Omnia Vincit Veritas."

"Wine is Strong; The King is Stronger; Women are Stronger Still; And The Truth Will Set You Free."

THIRTY ONE

"Baggage" Return

You have to become as sick of telling about your victimhood as we are of listening to it! That's the plain truth. It's just your story. Don't attach by repeating it constantly! I have had clients come to see me and tell me that they have been everywhere trying to "heal" their issues. They have even told me that they have been to see John of God (the renowned healer in Brazil) twice! My first thought is, "And you are coming to see me, because?"

These people are the ones I call Healer Hoppers. They go around the world seeing everyone they can, but only to show us all that their story is SO much worse than anyone else on the planet. No one can cure THEM and they have proven it! Avoid these people like the plague. They love having "pity parties" where a group of them can gather around and swap stories of how hard their lives are. I refuse to attach to their baggage. I have actually had some people show real anger (which is the real feeling hidden underneath their story) and storm out on me saying that they wouldn't stay as I would not attach to their tales of woe.

Firstly, please realize that your anger is an energetic fire which ceaselessly burns inside and will only harm the one carrying it in the end. The object of your anger probably could not care less and their life is moving along comfortably. Secondly, understand that all anger on the planet is fear based. Fear of losing or having lost something you feel or felt essential to your world. Thirdly, be aware that anger makes you weaker and vulnerable, not stronger and more confident. Lastly, admit that the anger is simply a validation of the story of your victimhood! Once you allow these truths to even begin to make sense, your anger is beginning to transmute itself and dissolve. There are many techniques being circulated helping us how to release our anger. I am well versed in many of them. This book is not about focusing on negative feelings, so we'll crash right through them now instead of doing months or years of self work!

However the first lesson to learn is not to attach to someone else's story of victimhood on any level. Attaching sympathetically can prove ultimately devastating for you! Let me explain. If everything is energy and has an energetic signature, then, what these people are doing, consciously or subconsciously, is unloading their negative accumulated energy on to you! I used to try to help everyone who came to me, however, all too often they walk away feeling much better (for a short while) and I was left feeling as though I had just been hit by a truck! Sound familiar? So, in effect, you could be walking around carrying anger, rage, fear, shame, guilt etc. which isn't yours!

This is a serious problem for today's children. Millions of them are extremely aware of their environment. They can feel all emotions around individuals or places. They often get accused of being "too sensitive." Just a reminder at this juncture. It's not the sensitive children (or adults) that are the problem on this planet is it? However, what happens is that, over time these kids collect emotional baggage from family, friends and everyone they meet. Some of them actually take it on board deliberately, thinking that is their job, to carry other people's pain, to fix things. In many cases families actually expect it of them! Often they actually feel guilty when someone still exhibits the same negative energies as before! Over time these children become overwhelmed by the sheer volume of negativity they have accumulated and begin to lose sight of their own identity and become prime candidates for aggression or addiction! So, if you have accumulated these types of energy I want you to understand two things. Firstly, all of the people whose energy you have taken on board can never get better and resolve their issues because you are holding their energy; and, secondly, you can't fix it because it's not yours! I have worked with kids as young as eight years old explaining this before it's too late for them and the gift they possess of reading emotions and feelings starts to overwhelm them and become a curse.

So, how do you get rid of this accumulated energy? Are you ready to release it? Do you have any reason (resistance) not to release it? Would you be happy if it could be done quickly and completely? Having recognized that this has been a trait of yours through life and that the only way to free yourself of it and to help others by returning what is rightfully theirs back to them, you simply sit quietly for a moment or two, eyes closed, taking a few slow, fairly deep breaths to calm and centre yourself. [I usually advise clients to actually pay attention to hearing the sound of these breaths.] Then you are ready. All that is required now is for you to say:

"I now understand and recognize that I have been carrying and accumulating many heavy and dense energies from many people and places for my whole life. I thought I was helping. I was mistaken. I now understand, that for healing to occur, for them and for me, I must return all such energies to their source. Therefore, to all people and places, remembered or forgotten, still with us or passed over, in all directions of time, I lovingly return what is rightfully yours. Aho."

Until you get used to holding your own space you may want to repeat that statement each night before sleeping and again before starting your day.

Next, take another two or three breaths, again hearing your breath, feeling how much lighter you are feeling and resolve never to accumulate physical or emotional pain from another ever again. It is NOT your role and in essence helps no one. Reject their negative energy no matter how hard they try to force it on you. Tell them this:

"I can stand beside you or behind you and encourage you and cheer for you on your journey through your issues, but I cannot and will not carry it for you ever again. It is yours and only you can resolve it."

It's that easy and simple and can be learned by anyone at any age.

Now to return to how you are going to deal with your deep, fear based, anger as we were discussing earlier in this chapter. You just dealt with it! As you return all the pain given to you by others, you will start to feel lighter again as you begin to touch the part of yourself that you thought you had lost forever. That apparent separation from yourself is actually the fear that created the anger within you.

I had an eight year old girl as a patient who wrote to me saying how much she loved releasing negativity. She thanked me for showing her how and she does it regularly, saying that, for her, it feels like all of the "bad stuff" is coming out through her toes and into the earth! This is her way of discharging all of the negative energy she unknowingly gathers from those around her each day. Many children (and adults) are susceptible to this and the technique known as "grounding" is an invaluable tool for them throughout their lives.

THIRTY TWO

Energetically Drained

People who are successful, prosperous and happy generally have a very practical and grounded approach to their lives. The vast majority of people who do not enjoy this type of life are generally not practical, logical or grounded in their thought patterns or their beliefs. They are ultimately tossed on the tide of whatever their environment tells them to be tossed on with no ultimate control of their destination on any level.

We have seen how other people can unload their negative energy on to us with devastating effect and have discussed how not to accept it. However, another tragic component for many people is that they allow others to actually take their energy and leave them drained! This form of vampirism is all too prevalent in many subtle and overt ways.

I have given examples of how some of the more sensitive among us can accumulate negative emotional energy from others and how to return it to them. Now we discuss deliberate energetic depletion or theft!

I have witnessed (and experienced) much damage being done to individuals who are unaware that they, by being disconnected to the earth energy, are dangerously vulnerable to psychic attack. [If anyone doesn't believe there is scientific proof of this energetic capability should watch movies like *Men Who Stare at Goats*]

On a personal level I have come to understand the need for regular grounding. Let me clarify what "grounding" is. Some people confuse it with meditation. Meditation is the practice of quieting the conscious mind. I have met many people who practice meditation religiously who are often far from being grounded. Don't misunderstand me, meditation is a powerful tool which I have studied in its various forms in achieving inner peace and prosperity but without grounding can often prove limited in its efficacy.

So what is grounding? Grounding, in essence, is connecting to the earth we walk on. When we are not "grounded" we walk with our "heads in the clouds" . . . "disconnected from reality" . . . "out of our body" . . . "spaced out" . . . to mention but a few familiar phrases. This state of disconnection is not a healthy place for anyone as I will show.

We are encouraged by the establishment to always "look up" for salvation, for your angels, for heaven, etc. Why do you think that is? It is another Lie That Binds us. How many of you could comfortably pray to the angels below you? I bet almost all of you feel uncomfortable with this thought. Quite surprising isn't it? Yet Indigenous societies always ceremoniously connected to the earth regularly to discharge negative energy and to receive positive energy.

In today's age of large conferences/gatherings and workshops I have encountered many energetic encounters of this kind. In fact I now clearly see that there are certain individuals who attend workshops and courses with any energetic or spiritual content with their only goal to be one of replenishing their own energy to the detriment of those they connect with. The most obvious "victims" for them are the clearly ungrounded individuals who attend these events "looking for their soul mate!" They search out everyone in the room deciding "Is it him?" or "Is it her?" and then they complain when their hearts get "broken" after a brief sexual encounter during the conference. Happens all the time and the predators are ready and waiting as that is exactly why they are there.

However, I have also known many fellow participants who go to these gatherings entirely ungrounded and hoping to find strength and instead leave even weaker. What do they do next? Thinking that they have somehow failed they return for more of the same! I have even heard some speakers tell participants that grounding is unnecessary and to stay disconnected!

This flies in the face of Indigenous Teachings on a global scale.

How can you ever reach the prosperity you desire when your energy is continually being siphoned off by others?

Whether I have convinced you or not, please believe that if you are grounded you are safe from energetic theft or attack. It's that simple.

How many of us know people who claim to be "healers" or "masters" particularly at Reiki, who are hardly great examples of a practical, balanced and successful life? They can be classic examples of being totally ungrounded, totally living in the energy of their upper energy centres or chakras with no connection to the earth energy or their own lower level energy centres. If you want to be successful and prosperous then practice grounding every day. It only takes 3 or 4 minutes and you will feel the difference every time you do it. There are many grounding "techniques" available. Find the one that is best for you. My protocol of choice has proven successful for people of all ages and backgrounds, so I will share it with you now for you to try if you so choose.

Preferably begin by standing with your feet comfortably apart and close your eyes. Now picture yourself standing on your favourite spot on the planet (even if you have never physically been there). Feel the earth, sand or rock under your feet. Know that this is the spot YOU have chosen and you are completely safe there. Now, with every in breath feel the sacred earth begin to fill your feet, then up through your legs, further with each in breath, like you were a syringe slowly filling. Smell that earth, feel the texture of it as it gradually fills you unconditionally and safely. When you fill completely, wait for a moment or two, then imagine a tube of gold or silver coloured liquid or light attaching to the top of your head, and, as you slowly exhale, feel that liquid entering through the top of your head, like a syringe being emptied and allow the liquid or light to begin to wash the earth back down, taking with it anything that does not best serve you in that moment. Feel that liquid rinsing out all of the main tracts and nooks and crannies within you with each exhalation until it begins to clear your ankles and feet. Then with each out breath continue to let the liquid or light follow down into the earth gradually forming a root system. Some roots may go deep, others spread out close to the surface. It's all good and will be different every time depending on how you are feeling. There is no wrong way to do this exercise. When you feel your roots are firmly connected to the earth, take a couple of slow deep breaths before opening your eyes, then simply carry on with your day.

Do this at home, on workshops, at school, and you will feel noticeably calmer and focussed—instantly. Then remember that being grounded like this is exactly what those who would keep you under control don't want you to understand and experience and incorporate it into your daily life in a practical and logical manner.

THIRTY THREE

Energetic Imprints

I hope that I can now help you to fully understand the need for, and the truth behind, the normal practice of clearing negative or heavy energy in your children, your home, or workplace. Once you understand that this is not magic, myth or miracle you can decide whether to develop those abilities in yourself or simply bring in someone who does this for a living. You have trusted me so far in this book. Drop your resistance just enough to allow me to de mystify this process also.

Clearing the land of negative or dense energy is something that has always been done by indigenous people around the planet and was (and still is) very effective. As modern science now admits, energy does attach to people places and things and can indeed be altered or moved on. Secondly, as science now also admits that there are many dimensions around us at all times the reality of the presence of spirits is now a scientific fact. You have thought that changing these energies was only for specialized people such as Priests, Witch-doctors, Shaman etc. I do not believe this to be necessarily true. I believe we are all capable of shifting the energies within ourselves and in our homes, our workplaces, places we frequent and even our country if we so choose. So, if this proves to be true, then another complete set of magic and miracles becomes your norm, as it did mine. Let me explain.

Most societies have a house warming party for people who move into their new home. This has always been so throughout the ages, however the part that has been forgotten is that prior to moving in, the Shaman or Priest/Priestess would first be brought into the home to clear any energies that existed there, either long term or from previous residents; then the new tenant's family and friends would come bearing happiness and good wishes for a house warming party which would impregnate the home with that energy so the new hosts could build their lives around that energy. Some religions, such as catholic, still ask the priest to come and bless their home, so the practice still persists just has been forgotten by most of us. I am asked, with increasing frequency now, to clear or settle the energy in home or commercial properties before new owners have their house warming or grand opening of their new business venture, as well as to clear existing businesses or homes which are clearly holding negative or dense energy.

On September 6th 1997, Lady Dianna was buried in a private vault on an island in the family estate of Althorp House in England. Seldom has the world joined in such unity in a day of mourning. I was told that shortly afterwards a group of well recognized Indigenous Shaman and Empathetic Psychics were given access to the area and their findings were quite startling. As they got closer to the burial site they all suddenly had tears streaming down their faces. As they stepped back a few meters, the tears stopped. They repeated the process several times with the results always being the same. It seemed that so much grief from around the world had been focused on that site that there was an actual accumulated energetic wall of sadness around the place, which would infer that the land does indeed hold energy projected to it as I have spoken about in earlier chapters.

This energy can be cleared anywhere simply by projecting the energy of compassion, love and happiness to the spot. Then have a party!!

However, while many are of the belief that clearing the land of energies is a complex and demanding task, I have found, for the most part, that, while it can indeed be demanding, it is always relatively straightforward and simple in its approach.

There are two factors to be considered as you will see. One is indeed the energy accumulated in the land and the other is the recognition of the presence of spirits which some call ghosts. Let me clarify with more examples.

In Mexico I was taken to a very revered spot in their history. It is in the State of Nayarit, near the city of Tepic. This spot is the scene of the tragedy that sparked the Mexican Revolution and changed the fabric of a nation. There is a large factory there, which was once the site of massed production of goods, and the workforce there suffered considerably. Work conditions were horrendous, disfiguring accidents and amputations were the norm, finally the workers began to rebel and protest for better, more humane, work conditions. The army was called in to quell the protests and eventually blood ran through the factory and the streets as the protestors were subdued. However, a flame had been lit here that became a wildfire as it spread across Mexico and the ultimately successful Worker's Revolution erupted.

So I was brought here by some highly respected business people to clear the energy at the heart of it all, which, of course, was in the abandoned factory itself.

It had been an impressive structure indeed in its day, but as I approached it I felt a growing sense of dread and horror as I tuned into the energy being held there. It is the only place I have been to where I honestly can say I felt more than a flicker of fear as I entered the deserted buildings and began to walk alone through the unlit corridors and massive areas that once held the factory production lines.

I had to stop frequently as I began to allow the trapped energy to flow again. Some spots were almost overwhelming. At one point, in a very long, wide and almost dark empty building I suddenly sensed something decidedly negative right behind me. It was so much bigger than me, almost filling the area behind me and its intent did not feel at all friendly. My neck and my back had become very cold. I did not know what it was, nor do I wish to know, however, I stood my ground, and without turning around, I continued with the clearing process, this time focusing entirely on the negative energetic. The coldness seemed to be increasing and then suddenly in a brief moment, the energy was gone, and my neck and back felt normal again! As I looked around I could see and feel that everything felt different and bright. I was able to finish my walk through the factory fairly quickly and under no duress whatsoever. I have no idea to this day exactly what I had encountered, but I do know for certain that it was the catalyst for everything that happened there, and when it left, the buildings and the land were healed. I asked God for a sign, as always, that my work had not been a figment of my imagination, and rejoined the group who were waiting for me almost anxiously at the front of the factory, and who seemed truly happy to see me again, as I was to see them.

The rest of the day passed in the company of friends and over the next two days I had not seen the sign I had asked for and therefore was unsure of what had been real or what had been imagined. I had not told any of my friends that I always asked for a sign, so I was delighted when one of them contacted me to say that they had information that they felt I should know. Apparently for one month prior to my visit the area had been experiencing earth tremors of increasing frequency and duration. I had not been made aware of this prior to this moment. This had been a cause of growing concern in the community. At exactly 2:22 p.m. as I exited the building the last tremor had been recorded and there had been no further tremors reported since. I advised them to have a party there to celebrate the removal of the old energy and to anchor in a new energy.

Hopefully the ripple effects of this change in energetic has spread far beyond the factory and even the community and has had a calming effect on the State of Nayarit, and even Mexico itself.

The Place of the Bones is an area on the Kona coast of Big Island, Hawaii. Many years ago there was a large settlement there. It became the place where the Indigenous Hawaiians made their last stand against those who were destroying their culture. Apparently there were thousands of bodies on the black lava rock beaches, eventually becoming a tangle of bleached bones, hence the name Place of the Bones. Some Hawaiians we met are at peace going to this spot, while others will not even get close to it, saying it is full of angry spirits.

I was brought down there by a acutely aware friend, along with my partner, on New Year's Eve to watch the sunset and to feel for myself what it was all about. It is a beautiful spot, black lava fields running to the shore, where rolling waves crash against them, sending spray high into the air, which seem to hang suspended, sparkling magically before shimmering down through the setting sunlight. There was not a breath of wind and I only felt a deep sense of peace there although I also sensed I was far from alone.

It is an incredible feeling to realize that you are probably the last person to see the sun set on Dec. 31st for the next people to see it, will see it as a sunrise (once again I had to pinch myself, reminding myself "I'm just a wee boy from Glasgow"). And so I said farewell to 2011 and looked forward to the coming year 2012.

I asked for a sign as always that what I was feeling was accurate, and began my work. I didn't feel that the land here needed energetic clearing! The peace I was feeling was coming from the land itself. Whatever tragedies had unfolded here had not diminished the natural loving and healing energy of this spot (one of many such places on Big Island). Why then did so many Hawaiians not come here? I think the story was put out to protect the area and to keep strangers, aka Haole (pronounced HowLee) away. I will explain the word Haole in a later chapter. The legend says that the spirits are there to protect the land. I got a very clear sense that the land was as beautiful as ever and did not require protecting on any level. So why were there so many "ghosts" here and such an underlying current of anger? It didn't make sense and I asked for answers which I suddenly realized had already been given to me by a good friend. She had told me that she had a vivid dream recently. In this dream she was being tortured. She remembers being filled with rage and spitting at her tormentors, determined that they would not kill her no matter what they did to her. The dream had been terrifyingly real to her and left her shaken. However it had not recurred and was simply a conversation piece between us. As I remembered her story, everything seemed to make sense. I realized that these men and women who died here were protecting their indigenous beliefs and refused to surrender them, even if it cost them their lives. They too would have felt like my friend in her dream; filled with hate for those who were killing the truth and they would swear that they would never leave that place, even after death. And so it was. I was then able to offer gratitude to these spirits for staying and holding the sacred space; then allowing them to release the anger they were holding as anger itself protects or heals nothing, then they were free to stay or move on as they chose.

I was again thoroughly filled with the feeling of love and compassion; similar to the one given by the psychic children, only amplified to a level I had never experienced before and I knew that I was on the right track.

So, was there a physical sign? Indeed there was and I have put the photograph into this book so you all can see for yourselves. This picture is completely as it first showed itself. You decide for yourself. Before doing my work in this sacred spot I had my picture taken on site with a Hawaiian friend, then she offered to take one of me and my partner. She didn't know how to operate the camera, so we showed her, aim and shoot, pointing the camera at the ground at our feet and pressing the shutter to demonstrate. When I down loaded the pictures later I almost deleted this blank shot automatically, until I clearly saw a skull, with eyes very much alive, staring up from the ground! There is more than that in the picture but the skull itself is undeniable. As I said, always ask for a sign and you will always be given one.

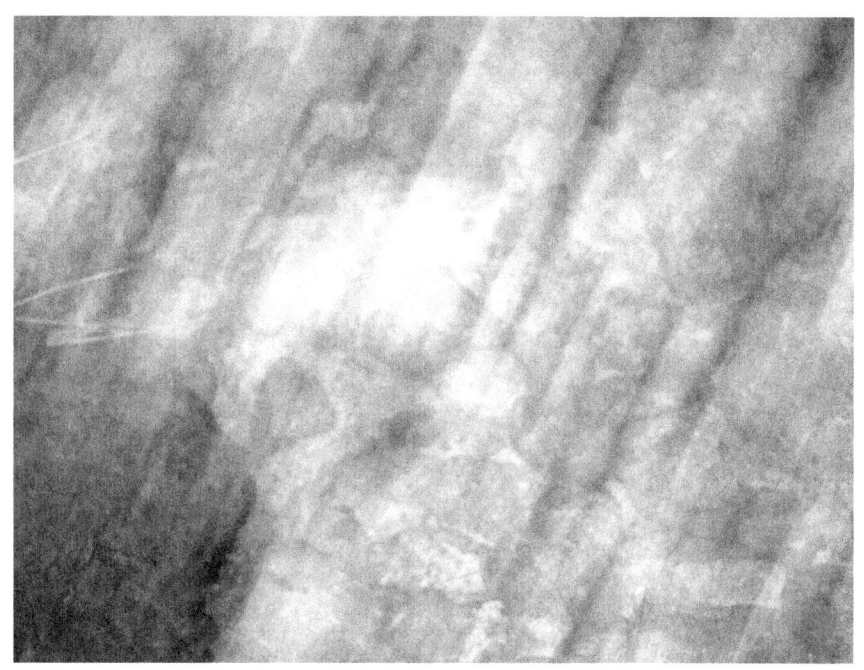

THIRTY FOUR

The Magic of Hawaii

The most isolated and possibly the most beautiful spot on the planet, with no land for over 2,000 miles in any direction, the Hawaiian chain of islands are still untouched by many of the obsessions of modern society and, I believe, no, I know, hold many a big key to the future of the planet. So much of their teaching is about keeping the memory of that magical part within us alive and well. The part we are calling The Unicorn.

The word Hawaii does not symbolize a place, it is a state of being! To Hawaiians, Ha = breath,

Everything is about breath to them, for without breath we do not live, and every breath is a sacred gift from Creator. With every breath we receive and give out life itself. Wai = fresh water, the god given life source of all things, without which nothing would survive and the letter I = a symbol for God. They have no name for God as they say there is no name for something which is omnipresent and omnipotent therefore just the symbol "I" is used. Therefore to live in Ha-wai-i is to live in a state of grace and gratitude for all life that comes through creator in the forms of breath and water. This gifts respect to all forms of nature and for each other. Therefore when Western man came along and repressed the natural ways the Hawaiians called them Haole, pronounced Howlee, which means Ha = breath, Ole = without, in other words we were clearly disconnected from all natural laws of existence and coexistence.

In their own words:

"Being Hawaiian is not just about a race of people. It is about the spiritual nobility of the soul, the living legacy of love/aloha, and the creative power/mana of manifestation that the ancestors gifted to us and left for us to uphold. It is about a state of the heart, a state of mind, a state of consciousness of good, and a state of oneness. We uphold this gift by understanding, contemplating and being Pono (*righteous*]) walking in the footsteps of na kupuna (*indigenous teachers*); na ancestors and na aumakua (*spirit guides*) in alignment with the Divine/ Ke Akua and in Harmonious Relations. All of humanity can benefit from these ancient cultural values of spiritual nobility, a way of Seeing, a way of Being, the Sacred Hawaiian Way in the Spirit of Pure Aloha.

We knew that the goal of life was to Honor All things Sacred and the Sacredness in All Things. To walk up the mountain of life protecting your Sacred Mana, your Aloha, your Sacred Bowl of Light, Malama Mana'o. Protect and take care of the Oneness, Harmony, Aloha of your Thoughts, your way of Seeing with the Heart, divorcing duality and only Seeing Oneness. Ku'ialua, Hawaiian martial art is the practice of power over Death and Destruction. Ku'ialua understands the mind-Mana'o is your first and best weapon or your worst enemy.

Every thought, feeling, perception, spoken word, and performed action impregnates the universe. It is never forgotten and it is never overlooked. The universe is always vibrationally mathematically exacting in its law of attraction. The thought vibrational resonances are carried in your sacred bowl of light, so Malama, take great care" from *The Subtle Sacred Secrets of Aloha* by Kahu Kahealani Kawaiolamanaloa Satchitananda.

Holding the vibration of the Law of Creation in gratitude presents us with the abundance, peace and harmony we desire and deserve, which is exactly what you have seen presented throughout this book!

It was six years ago now when we found ourselves at the entrance to the Valley of The Kings on Big Island, Hawaii, at midnight, under an August full moon. We were privileged to be there under the protection of a revered leader and kahuna. Just beyond where we stood there were Hawaiian warriors, powerful young men with tremendous energy and vitality who were ensuring that no one passed beyond them into the valley below. We were very content just to be that close to what was unfolding below us in the Valley. That night there was a gathering of over 5,000 warriors, young men and women from every walk of life.

However, although the meeting was indeed private and secret, the agenda was not one to cause concern. They were there to perform the ancient ceremony of Ho'oponopono; the ceremony of forgiveness. For those who do not know what that is; it is a powerful personal cleansing tool which affects all things. It has been presented to the United Nations and has gained global recognition in the past three years. The Hawaiians were practicing the concepts of today's psychology such as Freud and Neuro Linguistic Programming thousands of years before they showed up on modern western man's radar. So what is Ho'oponopono? It is about forgiveness of all people and all things, including ourselves. It is simply four short phrases, "I'm sorry, Please forgive me, I love you, Thank you." Directed at whomever you wish to be at peace with. What you are saying is "I am sorry for all of the PERCEIVED wrongs that you feel I have done to you" . . . "Please forgive me, I love you, thank you." Very simple and powerful words when said sincerely. The other party does not have to be present for it to be effective. Many scenarios and relationships have been healed, some instantly by these words. So here were 5,000 young men and women practicing Ho'oponopono, asking forgiveness first from and to parents, spouses and children, then between families, then between the individual islands, then from the Islands to and from the mainland U.S.A. They were clearing any negative vibrations they were holding towards anyone and everyone, thus raising and purifying their own vibration in the process. We were deeply touched by the sincerity of these young people; determined to take back ownership of their lands, which had been taken by force and without any treaty, a land where the people to this day have not been given even the Indigenous People Rights afforded to Native American Indians! There must be absolute terror in the hearts of those imposing themselves in this way on these loving people! They fear that giving them any kind of status would encourage the release of The Unicorn amongst them! That suppression should be a big clue for us all! Please spare a loving thought of Aloha to the Hawaiian people as you read this.

However, as these young ones showed, The Unicorn is indeed alive and well and is being remembered and released by ever increasing numbers of Hawaiians through protocols such as Ho'oponopono. How perfect are they, when in a situation which begs for anger and redress of wrongs imposed on them, these young people are deliberately clearing these emotions before embarking peacefully on their mission to reclaim their land. You should practice it whenever you find yourself in any conflict, the results will often amaze you!

The Hawaiians, like many young people around the globe, have deliberately been disconnected from their ancient roots, leaving them feeling exactly that—disconnected and alone. There is a story of how they deal with these issues which many other societies would do well to copy. There were a group of young teenagers there who were becoming more disconnected all the time, with their behaviors moving from anti social to the edge of being criminal. A well respected leader and Kahuna, known affectionately as Papa K, went into the school where these young men were attending and told them they were leaving with him for two weeks. They asked him what were they going to do? He replied that they were going to talk, think, eat and breathe in Hawaiian. They laughed at Papa saying they didn't speak Hawaiian. He smiled and simply said "You will." The camp they took the boys to was manned by some of the warrior men and women I spoke of earlier and for two weeks the lads were definitely in Hawaiian Immersion. At the end of the two weeks, the youths came out of the camp singing an ancient Hawaiian chant and the fascinating thing was that the parents and grandparents awaiting them burst into tears on hearing this. As far as I know, none of the boys has been in serious trouble since that time of reconnection to their roots. Papa K knew why they felt disconnected. When he was only 10 years old, he was overheard speaking in Hawaiian and was imprisoned for two weeks for his "crime." He understood the ways of the invaders who systematically eliminate all traces of a culture, banning their clothing, language, customs and beliefs and forcefully inserting their own "Lies That Bind" them from that day on. Children everywhere should be reconnected to their ancestral heritage which is in their blood and is part of their genetics. It should be mandatory in education. I believe that teenage crime, drug abuse, violence and suicides would reduce dramatically if the children once again had a knowledge and pride in their heritage. I believe that this connecting to their roots is the key to releasing the innate power within them which the rulers fear so greatly. From that point on the Law of Creation will manifest for them as it does for you.

For those of you who understand that some parts of this planet have more active energy than others, then I know you will understand when I tell you that Big Island is all about base energy. In simple terms, your shit will undoubtedly surface here! If you don't want to deal with your issues then don't come around Big Island. On a physical level there is such a high accumulation of iron in the ground here that even the space satellites realign their GPS when passing over it! There are hundreds of miles of underground passageways and caverns of lava tubes on Big Island, some of which are so ionized that no bacteria can grow there. These then would have been perfect spots for those injured in combat to be hospitalized so their wounds could heal!

My partner and I often smile as we see (or hear) couples clearly not getting along as their issues bubble up to the boil. In effect, if you recognize it for the healing release it actually is and understand how good that is for you, then just let it come and work with the flow without attaching to it, the unsettled energy in you will clear quickly. If not it's going to be long hard emotionally painful ride. I have now been to the Big Island on twelve different occasions over the years and can unequivocally vouch that this land is only for those brave enough to allow whatever needs to move on to transmute accordingly. Even the athletes seem to understand this now. Kona is the home of the legendary Iron Man Triathlon and every year athletes from around the globe gather for this extreme demanding event. Many mainstream athletes now arrive some time before the event and tune in to connect to the land there and to make offering to Madame Pele, the Fire Goddess to ask for her blessing.

I have seen many "miracles" on the Big Island, some of which confuse me to this day, but I know I will understand them if and when I am supposed to and I let it go at that. Some examples?

I had a gash on my knee from the coral. My Hawaiian companions put a plant leaf on it, along with other remedies, and told me to leave it on for a while. When I took the leaf off three hours later the cut was gone. Not just healed, completely gone!

I have seen a kahuna stand by a large lagoon and gently call to the sea turtles there and instantly their heads have popped up in response all around the bay!

I have witnessed where the tsunami from Japan tore its way down the west coastline of Big Island, obliterating houses and resorts yet leaving the Heiaus (*sacred spots*) completely intact! This would necessitate the tsunami almost making a U turn to take out the target areas and leave the rest. It doesn't make sense, even as you look at the scene.

I have seen individuals, collecting Abalone shells from high surf areas, talk or pray to the water first and watched in amazement as the waters seemed to redirect themselves just long enough for them to walk down and collect specific shells, and as they walk away, the waves return in the pattern as before!

I have stood on the live volcanic rim of Kilauea and make offering to Pele, the Goddess there. I felt myself being pulled into the crater far below me, and I'm sure would indeed have been drawn in but somehow felt myself being pulled back to safety. My partner spoke in amazement of how, as I got to the edge, the Kahuna's assembled about ten meters behind me, had all dropped on to one knee and each had their arms extended as though they were energetically pulling me back!

What is a Kahuna you may ask? That almost defies definition however, in essence a Kahuna is one who is a keeper of the wise and hidden secrets. Kahunas are trained in knowing God in everything. The Kahuna therefore is "a calm, high servant of those who may be seeking higher emotional evolution. Like all true leaders and healers, a Kahuna serves their community. Some were healers, others heads of sacred dance or Hula, or of martial arts, others were considered sorcerers." from The Wise Secrets of Aloha by Kahuna Harry Uhane, Jim and Garnette Arledge.

Had I not seen these, and many other, things for myself on Big Island, I would not have believed them, so I have simply related them to you now as part of my truth, that you may decide for yourself.

I am extremely pleased that my workshop KCR has been accepted by them and actively being promoted by them! I have been blessed by seeing some of them as my clients when I am there and will nourish the relationship in whatever way proves to be best for them.

THIRTY FIVE

The Hula

I am not Hawaiian. Therefore I do not put myself out there as any sort of teacher of Hawaiian ways. I simply, with deep love and appreciation, share what I have been led to understand and so believe. Beyond and more powerful than any martial art, there is the Hula! Yet another gift from Hawaii to the world. By this I do not mean the coconut shell bikini top and grass skirt image perpetuated by Hollywood. I was privileged to attend one evening at the Merry Monarch Hula Festival in Hilo, Hawaii a year ago. Added to that we were blessed to stay in a beautiful home there, in the company of several Kapuna and Kahuna who I am now truly humbled and grateful to call my friends. The food and conversation were just perfect and many treatments were exchanged between us. These lovely ladies had gone into the mountains to collect thousands of fresh flowers and they spent many hours making beautifully colored and fragrant garlands (leis) for around our necks and on our heads. This food, treatments, conversation and making the leis was all gradually increasing our vibration of compassion and gratitude and, in essence was putting us in the correct frame of mind and heart for the Festival itself. We were not the only ones preparing for or being prepared for a role in the community heart space of this gathering.

The Merry Monarch Festival is the Perpetuation, Preservation and Promotion of the art of Hula and the Hawaiian Culture. All of their loving and beautiful truths remain alive here, surviving the attempts at genocide and the destructive "Lies That Bind" perpetuated upon them.

This Festival is indeed a loving connection to their roots, their ancestry and is an anchor for their future and a beacon to their youth.

Ancient Hawaiians had no written language. Instead, all communication beyond the spoken word took place in the form of chants and the dance called hula. Hula and its accompanying chants recorded Hawaiian genealogy, mythology, and prayers of the heart and mind. The hula was the means by which the culture, history, stories and almost every aspect of Hawaiian life was expressed and passed down through generations. It was banned for over seventy years by Christian missionaries. The chants had incredible power too. It is the power of the Hawaiian language itself, which still terrifies those who control them so much, that even the Hawaiian language being taught in University today is NOT the authentic language with some letters being deliberately removed to disempower the vibration!

Because the Merrie (*Merry*) Monarch Festival has maintained strict standards of authenticity, the true history and culture of the ancient Hawaiian people is being perpetuated. Without such educational and cultural organizations as the Merrie Monarch Festival, the history and unique traditions of the Hawaiian people will be lost forever.

In preparation for the Merrie Monarch Festival, hula studios and instructors in Hawaii and on the U.S. Mainland hold classes, workshops, and seminars throughout the year to teach the art of hula, the meaning of Hawaiian chants and songs, the Hawaiian language, the making of Hawaiian clothing and crafts, and the history of the Hawaiian people.

Through this ongoing year-round learning process, students also gain a knowledge and appreciation of the unique harmony and balance the ancient Hawaiian people maintained with their island environment. The chants, songs and dance tell stories of the Hawaiians' relationship with nature-the birds and fish, trees and flowers, mountains, oceans, rivers, wind, rain and Hawaii's active volcanoes.

You should now be able to sense this focused gathering of love gaining momentum as participants and audience begin to gather on Big Island.

The Festival has taken the form of a competition where music, chanting and hula are the main contenders. The Hawaiian language is recognised as having a high vibrational healing tone component, as does the Hula, so the environment is truly magical. All you have to do is breathe it in and release it with gratitude. The competition is, on one level, superfluous.

The energy created there is indeed a sacred, magical and mystical thing.

I am still in gratitude for the privilege of being allowed to participate in this gathering of pure Aloha.

My research has shown me that, when the hula is performed at the highest levels it transcends all martial arts! Those who seek constant improvements in these fields at the highest levels are eventually made aware of this. The Hula in its purest form creates such an energetic of pure love and light that negativity of any form, which is a lower vibration, simply cannot enter. The Hula was not only a dance for the females (Wahine). The Hula had various forms and was standard male (Kane) training also.

The word Hula itself means "Work with the light" or "Talk to God." In such a state of connection no harm could come. Sounds like magic and miracles, myths and legends stuff does it not? As you free The Unicorn within you, you will come to realize that it is an undeniable truth. The Hawaiians were not the only ones who knew this "secret." Other Indigenous people knew this also. For example, when Native American Chiefs such as Crazy Horse or Geronimo would ride with arms outstretched across the battle line and not be hit by gunfire, even rapid fire Gatling guns did not injure them, they were not doing this as an act of ego or an act of antagonism to the enemy. It was a display to both sides that the answer was not in combat but in inner peace and compassion, connected to your higher spirit, from which place no violence was possible. The Whirling Dervish Sufi Dancers also create this reality. However it is my belief that Hula contains all components of Hawaiian beliefs and is the central vessel of survival and perpetuation of the people and possibly the planet.

Just last year, my partner and I were invited to attend a true hula class and we set up two treatment tables in the room. As the ladies danced, as they were drawn they would leave the group and come to one of our tables and receive my KCR protocol, then return to the dance to see how it had affected them. All reports were most positive. The energy in that room on that evening was what I can best describe as thundering compassion, completely irresistible, and I am deeply honoured at having been allowed to experience it.

I have seen some people today still achieve this to some degree in Western Society. An example is James Twyman, the Peace Troubadour, with whom I studied over a two year period, culminating in my receiving my certification as an Ordained Minister of Spiritual Peacemaking. Jimmy has travelled to almost all of the battle torn centers on the planet, preaching peace, and has never once been put in danger of his life often in the middle of armed conflict!

I believe that Jimmy puts himself into that state of high vibration in these scenarios and, in his own words, is uncovering the peace which lies beneath all conflict.

Jimmy has had incredible interactions with today's psychic children over the years, and it was these stories that first attracted me to his work. If you remember all of the stories I have told throughout this book of my interactions with these kids you will realize that there is a common thread in them all. I don't hear words of communication from them, yet I am left with such a deep feeling of peace after every contact. I finally get it! This is what they bring! Their gift is the ability to transmit pure unconditional love and awaken the deep inner peace that exists inside everyone. They awaken The Unicorn! It is the same feeling as is experienced by the energy of Hula. The children's message to humanity is simple. We have simply forgotten our potential and have become chained by the "Lies that Bind." Recognize the illusion and create your future. The question/statement they make to each of us is this

"How would you behave if you knew that you are an Emissary of Light?" . . . "BEGIN"

We can all create this feeling of peace within us if we truly believe (or remember) that we can. When I ask myself, what is it that I want today, the deep answer is simply Peace, internally and externally. My intent therefore is clear. How the Universe intends to provide it is of no interest to me. I have made a clear request to the Law of Creation and, with more and more frequency it is being manifested.

This is how you create peace in your personal life and in your business world. Others around you will either move into a similar vibration or will move away from it! The next time someone is arguing with you, whether in family or business circumstances, allow yourself to see the light inside them that they cannot see in themselves. Stay focussed on it and do not react to their provocative and unreasonable behaviour. Within minutes they will calm down or will storm out of the room. Either way you will feel empowered and at peace! This approach works every time. Practice it when you are amongst others on a bus, train or in a restaurant and you will become acutely aware of the changes happening around you. It is the same in business. If you create a world of true freedom that is full of compassion for others and have an attitude of service to humanity rather than one of competitiveness, you will attract way more business than you can handle, and will only attract those with a similar mindset, or should I say heartset. Feeling the freedom to create an environment where you are grateful for everything and open to receiving gratitude in return and your prosperity is guaranteed.

THIRTY SIX

Learn to Heal Yourself!

Instant self healing from physical issues is not only possible it is scientifically proven but they just haven't told you of the secret system inside you that can accomplish this! Tom was sent to see me for physical therapy, complaining of a stiff neck and shortage of breath. He had suffered from it for three months after a freak accident in his driveway. He owned a large pick up truck, complete with the mag wheels and all the chrome additions that are so popular and enjoyed by young men in Western Canada. One day, he was working on his truck, lying underneath it, when it somehow slipped into gear and rolled forward, the front tire rolling across his left shoulder, diagonally down across his rib cage, before thudding off of him on to the concrete driveway and stopping again! I understood exactly what was actually happening to him, thanks to my CTR training and decided on my approach accordingly. As he lay face up on my treatment table, while I sat at the head of the table with my hands cupping his neck and gently working with the muscles there, I asked him if the incident had been an unnerving experience. He replied that it was terrifying; that he could still visualise the wheel rolling over him; that he could still distinctly smell the tire. He said he was just lucky that the wheel had not run over his skull as it would have crushed him like an egg! I quietly waited for a moment then I gently asked him, that if what he said was true, then how come the wheel hadn't even broken a rib? Tom went dead still and quiet as my words impacted him, then, after a few seconds, I could feel a tremor building up inside his chest, until he began to shake visibly and almost violently while he also began sweating profusely! The tremors continued for around three minutes then slowly settled back down and stopped again. When Tom finally felt OK enough to sit back up he was very confused initially but also stunned to find that his stiff neck had fully resolved and he was pain free with full range of motion, for the first time since the accident. He had healed himself in three minutes!

Now let me explain what had happened as you learn how to heal YOUR self.

To learn to heal yourself you have to understand that there is a massive physical system throughout your body that you have never been told about! I know that sounds incredible but it is an absolute truth! Connective Tissue is the missing link to your physical healing! It is the holder of magic and miracles, the physical component of The Unicorn which till now has been chained and hidden within your body.

The largest system in the human body, connective tissue, also known as Fascia or Myofascia has the inherent capability to save your life or, if left untended, to limit both your life quality and duration. Yet it is altogether ignored in medical training . . . in fact students are told just to tear it out and throw it in the garbage when dissecting corpses as it has no purpose! The largest living system in the body has no purpose? It's like how we're told we have junk DNA! Does that attitude make any sense whatsoever? I do not believe that anything on earth has been created without purpose including DNA or connective tissue, so just so what is it that is being so deliberately hidden from us here? The simple truth will astound you.

Understand now that there is a web of tissue throughout your whole body, called connective tissue, that those who teach us "The Lies That Bind" are absolutely terrified you will uncover! Understanding this tissue and its purpose will empower you forever.

This web is easily viewed on dissection however does not show up on any standard medical scan such as X-rays, CT Scans, M.R.I's, etc. leading to many misdiagnosed patients and many others being told there is nothing wrong with them, that they are malingering or their symptoms are all in their minds!

I have had Medical Consultants attend my classes in this and, on day one, openly mock me. By Day 2 they are true believers and are shaking their heads in disbelief that they have never been taught this in all of their years at Medical School! Thanks to the groundbreaking work, in the face of incredible resistance, of pioneers such as John F, Barnes P.T. (remember him from my visualisation of Hawaii?) and others there are now over 60,000 practitioners trained in this field. For those interested in learning to be a practitioner I recommend John's website at www.myofascialrelease.com.

However, I strongly feel that this should NOT be the domain of the chosen few, so to speak. THE KNOWLEDGE OF CONNECTIVE TISSUE AND ITS EFFECTS ON THE HUMAN BODY SHOULD BE TAUGHT AS A BASIC HUMAN RIGHT AND BE TAUGHT AS PART OF HEALTHCARE IN SCHOOLS. There is no compromise to be made on this stance whatsoever.

Once people understand what it is and what it does they can correct many issues themselves, and, if not, can then access one of the trained practitioners for appropriate treatment. This is why I teach it to everyone as part of my Level 2 workshop, regardless of their medical or non medical background.

Let me now prove all of my claims to you beyond any reasonable doubt.

Firstly, I do not like the name Myofascia as it means nothing to the general public and also would indicate by the prefix Myo that it has something to do with muscles, which is completely incorrect. Therefore I will always relate to it as Connective Tissue as that is easy for the public to grasp and describes its function perfectly. Further, I do not subscribe to the treatment of the web as Myofascial Release (MFR) I refer to it as Connective Tissue Release (CTR).

So we have a web of tissue completely connecting every structure in your body like a meshwork with liquid in the mesh. If you think of a honeycomb you get the exact idea of what it looks like, or a sponge with the spaces all filled with liquid honey. It surrounds and interconnects every muscle, ligament, organ and nerve in your body. In more recent times, with the use of electron microscopes, scientists have shown that the web gets finer and finer, surrounding every individual muscle fibre, then every cell in the human body, and now admit that within the nucleus of each cell is that same living web! The function of the web is firstly, to deliver nutrition to every cell in your body. Next it is the major means of internal communications we possess, an incredible information highway, receiving and sending thousands of messages throughout the body every second of your life. Thirdly, it is a life protecting shock absorber, capable of withstanding incredible pressures when we are traumatised physically (or even emotionally). There is so much more to this magical system, however, for this book we will keep our approach focussed and simple and clarify what had happened to Tom.

The body's first reaction to stress is fight or flight. Most of us know that when threatened we can either run away quite quickly, driven by adrenaline, or we will fight with unusual strength . It is our body's way of surviving and has been our first line of defence since our cave man days. Interestingly enough it is no longer going to save us as a species. This was made clear in the tragedy that was 911. The apparent biggest threat ever seen on homeland soil unfolded in front of the whole world on live television. People either could not watch it at all or were drawn to watch it over and over in total disbelief. The normal response for mankind to go into fight or flight mode, for the first time in history is quite useless. There is no one to fight (as we know now over 10 years of trying and being absolutely no safer now than then) and there is nowhere to run as nowhere can truly be considered as safe anymore. So mankind will have to find another solution somehow and that is the real challenge.

However, there is a secondary line of defence that is being ignored by the medical profession completely. Imagine you are sitting in your car at a stop light and, glancing in your rear view mirror, you see a large truck bearing down on you at some speed and you know you are about to be hit from behind! You cannot run or fight, so, instantly the next line of defence kicks in. You freeze! Everything tenses as you brace yourself for the impact. The muscles and ligaments tighten up to take the impact, but the connective tissue web instantly solidifies to form a framework to protect you ! Some short time after the accident you start to shake and tremble. This in itself is not an indication of shock although should never be ignored as a possibility. The shaking is usually the body's way of the connective tissue coming out of the freeze response and now thawing again, returning to the pre stress or pre accident state.

In Tom's case, like millions of others, his connective tissue instantly freezing solid protected him from injury as the truck rolled over his ribcage, but he had never allowed it to thaw or relax (because he didn't know he could!) and therefore presented with the problems he had developed since. As soon as he became aware in his conscious mind that indeed something must have happened to protect him, the connective tissue was triggered to thaw or relax and he was healed. Just understanding this natural process can save millions of lives and end many disabilities. If all trauma, physical and emotional, is physically frozen in the connective tissue system then all the physical treatment, medication and counselling in the world will be limited in value until we are given permission to shake (thaw)!

I have stood in front of groups of young boys, aged twelve and thirteen, and asked them how many ever get into a fight in school. Most raise their hand. Then I ask them, how many of their knees or hands start to shake a short time after the fight is over. A few honest hands tentatively are raised while the rest simply avoid eye contact with me. Next I ask them how do they feel about that trembling? The answer they gave me rocked me to the core. "Coward," was the first thing they said, with heads around the room nodding in tacit agreement!

Here are a cross-section of societies young boys growing up thinking they are cowards! The lifelong ramifications to them and those around them could be horrific indeed. So I proceeded by asking them how would they feel if they knew that, not only was the shakiness normal but that it was the smart thing to do? Their faces literally lit up with excitement at the prospect. I then give examples of how animals, such as horses, will often tremble violently for a minute or two after being rescued from a ditch, then relax and run around as though nothing ever happened. That is the animal's connective tissue thawing or relaxing back to normal.

So these boys go home that night, knowing that they have connective tissue, knowing what it does, and for the rest of their lives they will understand and allow their body to tremble when necessary and will teach their children to do the same.

Recognize that when connective tissue tightens protectively and is not allowed to relax again that the cumulative effects of this can be at least, debilitating, and at worst deadly. When connective tissue tightens protectively it has been proven to do so with a force of up to two thousand pounds per square inch! If this is not relieved can you imagine the potential long term consequences?

I stopped my easily identifiable, bright orange pick up truck to help at a traffic accident close to my workplace one workday. One vehicle had a driver who had mild head wound and several people were around his vehicle. The other vehicle driver was a lady sitting staring straight ahead, window rolled down (it was a very hot day) and no one was looking after her. I went over to her and asked if she was OK? She nodded, still staring straight ahead. I then told her that I was just going to stay with her until the paramedics arrived, was that OK? Again she nodded in agreement. Next I told her that it was OK if she felt like shaking. Once again I was given a nod that she had heard me. I waited for a few minutes and as soon as the paramedics arrived and started talking with her, I left and continued back to work. I had quite forgotten about it all until, some months later, my office manager came back to my office to tell me of a call she had just received. She said the call was from a lady who claimed she was a driver of a vehicle that had been involved in an accident and that I had stopped to help her.

She had tracked me down by identifying my truck, parked outside of my clinic. She never left her name, but wanted to say thank you to me for stopping and staying with her until help arrived and also to say thank you to me for giving her permission to shake!

Surely this info should be headline news in every channel and newspaper and should be taught in every school on the planet? So why is this info being suppressed? I think that by now you will have a good grasp on the answer to this one.

But, at least, now that YOU understand how it works, then this vital and till now hidden part of your inner Unicorn has been unleashed and can never be told otherwise again!

Let each and every one of you now and always, take your power into your own hands, give yourself permission to tremble or shake as and when necessary and let your healing begin! It will happen when it is time, just relax and breathe into that truth. Namaste.

THIRTY SEVEN

Uncovering the Peace in Any Conflict

Uncovering the peace in any conflict. If your family conflict seems beyond repair, think again. As James Twyman teaches, a peacemaker is not one who creates peace in a situation. It is someone who uncovers the peace which already exists beneath the pain. Here is an example from my life experience of this philosophy.

I was asked to help a family end their conflict with one another. They thought they were dysfunctional! I have to laugh at that. They were well within the parameters of normalcy in my mind, with issues that many families have to face and deal with or bury and pretend everything is ok. In fact the most dysfunctional family I ever saw was probably the TV family "The Walton's." No one ever got angry with anyone else; white picket fence; home cooking; everything perfect. "Good night, John Boy" used to do my head in!

So, in my capacity as an Ordained Minister of Spiritual Peacemaking, before I agree to mediate in family disagreements there are some ground rules that they have to agree to.

1. Everyone has to be together at least fifteen minutes before the agreed start time.
2. No one leaves till it is over.
3. We all eat together afterwards, can be prepared beforehand or we can order in pizza.
4. Only one person can talk at a time. No Interrupting.
5. All comments have to be said while looking directly at me. Do not look at the person you are talking about.

So, in essence, I become like a lightning rod for the energies of the meeting. I have an object which we call the "talking" stick. Only the one holding the stick can talk. When they are finished, I take it back and see who asks for it next.

I make it clear beforehand that this is not a meeting to sort out winners and losers. That attitude will simply deepen the wounds one way or another and will prove totally counterproductive in the end.

When I arrive, I am usually made very welcome and I can feel the tension in the air. I make sure we're all comfortable and no one needs to visit the washroom etc, then we get straight into why we are here and what we hope to achieve. In the preliminaries I have made a point of seeing the light of perfection, the hidden unicorn, in each one of them, that they have forgotten about or are unable to accept in themselves. I actually already know that all will end well, as it has been my experience that anyone who genuinely doesn't want to make peace, who is too strongly connected to their victim story, will not show up at the meeting. All people in the room have a genuine desire for peace in the family, even although they may have strong views one way or another. This particular family are a truly beautiful and courageous group of souls, the children had grown together under the bipolar and often illogical, and even violent actions of an alcoholic parent. The parent had eventually left home, gone into rehab, made a full recovery, returned to a normal life, remarried and was living hundreds of miles away. That parent was fine and should be congratulated. However, as is often the case in these scenarios, the family that was left behind were still a deeply fractured unit. They were angry, frustrated, full of blame of each other, had deep feelings of inadequacy, ashamed of the traumas that had permeated their youth, having great difficulty forming romantic relationships, etc. Although they still met regularly, visiting and chatting as though everything was perfect, the visits were getting fewer and further between as the past began to surface. It was the now adult daughter, probably the one had been most deeply affected, who had decided that enough was enough and had asked the family to gather together and to allow me to be there. The fact that they agreed proved that they truly cared enough to try.

The talking stick was passed around as each one said who they were and why they thought they were here, including me, then we got down to the business at hand. Then the daughter took the stick and always looking directly at me, as required, spoke for a long time on what her memories were. The others then all took their turn. It was clear that everyone saw the scenario from different perspectives. However, when eventually, an adult son took the stick, and, again looking only at me, said that he had no idea his sister had endured those things, or that she had been so deeply affected by the turmoil in their home, the tears in his eyes betraying his own pain, I knew we were beginning to break down the walls between them. It's a fact that the problem is never what families think it is. Never. It all began with the fingers of judgement being pointed at the now recovered parent (who was not invited to the meeting) but gradually the underlying layers of anger at each other began to surface. This is when it is important that they do NOT look at each other when speaking, keeping all energy directed at me. Once the anger had actually surfaced, without interruption, and everyone began to feel as though they were actually being heard, then compassion and support for each other began to surface and the whole mood of the evening began to noticeably lighten. Gradually everyone's posture began to relax as the "elephant in the room" had been identified and could now be dealt with, uncovering the peace which had always been there under the elephant. The tears had changed to smiles and it was time to order pizza! They knew they still had a lot of talking to do to recover fully but the door was open now for this to happen. The last I heard they were all doing well, enjoying successful personal relationships and still open enough to put their feelings clearly on the table when they needed to. Of course, as you all now know, they could all just have done Ho'oponopono and saved themselves a lot of time, however for many families the tool of mediation is the only way they can accept.

The same principles can be successfully applied to small or even large corporations. The people who need to leave, or be asked to leave, generally are the ones who don't come to the meeting or do not adhere to the rules of conduct.

Anyone can in essence mediate in this way, however, I would definitely suggest some form of background in mediation before embarking on this course of action. It is imperative that the "mediator" is not a family member or an employee, they would be too involved personally and emotionally which would make them vulnerable and ineffective, and secondly, the mediator has to make it clear that they have no opinion to offer, even when asked for one. Calm, focussed and neutral at all times is the only route to success, taking nothing said personally and always focussing on the light within each speaker that they cannot see in themselves.

Another application of this became evident a few years ago when we met and befriended another wonderfully compassionate corporate lady in Calgary just starting out her new business venture, who has now created scenarios whereby people can uncover and connect to the forgotten magic and peace of The Unicorn in one another and, thanks to her, their divorcing and disconnection was a tolerable, and often peaceful, scenario with minimum impact on the children. Her compassionate approach to uncovering the peace in any conflict has created a large demand for her services and she is now franchising throughout North America and eventually Europe!

I will not tell the rest of my friend, Karen Stewart's story here, but you will enjoy reading of her success for yourself at Fairway Divorce Solutions where she is the Founder/CEO.

By being at peace and believing that the miracle of peace is always close at hand—true healing and harmony occur every time.

Let me now end this chapter with a quote which I wish I had known and understood when I was ten years old, one which would have prevented me from making my "fateful" decision.

May its simple and powerful truth resonate deeply in your mind and your heart, and release the light of The Unicorn within you to burst free, surrounding you instantly and forever.

"When you know yourself, you know the truth. When you refuse to know yourself, panic sets in as you seek a substitute. Terror pursues you when you realise you can never replace the eternal, and fear seizes you when you experience guilt for trying. The idea that we are alone and separate is just that—an idea, a thought. It is not true. The truth in you has fallen asleep and is having a dream of separation. But the dream is almost over." ~James Twyman

THIRTY EIGHT

The Secret of All Secrets!

The secret of all secrets! Now let me prove what it is that makes The Unicorn so feared by those who control you. To do so I will compare the "myth" of The Unicorn in history to the science of today. I want to discuss the work of Dr. Emoto, an eminent Japanese scientist.

He has proven beyond question that water connects to the vibration of everything around it, and let's remember that the earth's surface is over 70% water. He has also proven that the intent of spoken or written words can and does influence the crystalline structure of water in healthy or unhealthy ways. His phenomenal work is easily found for those who wish to learn more. Indeed I am delighted to share that I have been accepted for his Instructor Training in the near future.

He has proven that simply by saying the words I Love You to water produces beautiful crystalline formations. He has shown that the intent of love itself can reclaim rancid waterways, even when done from a distance!

Now let us consider that the human body is also composed of a high percentage of water. Think how all of the negative thoughts we have about ourselves, or imposed on us by others, must create unhealthy states in our body! Yet thinking only love about ourselves consistently will resolve this!

So, let me now remind you of the definition of The Unicorn I gave at the beginning of this book.

"The Unicorn is a legendary animal resembling a white horse with a spiralling horn projecting from its forehead. First mentioned by the ancient Greeks it became the most important 'real or imaginary?' animal throughout the Middle Ages. Commonly described as a SYMBOL OF PURITY AND GRACE, whose magical 'third eye' horn, HAD THE POWER TO PURIFY POISONED WATER AND TO HEAL ALL SICKNESS!"

And what is that power now proven to do just that? The power of love! So it is the power of love within each of us that must be kept chained by the controllers, as they know they are powerless once it is free again. And so it is.

Epilogue

As we come to the end of our journey together I sincerely ask you to allow yourself to breathe deeply and, taking a moment, actually allowing yourself to feel my open gratitude and love for journeying along with me through this book. Hold this feeling and then allow yourself to also enjoy the wave of gratitude gently moving into you from those in your world who are already raising their vibration, consciously or subconsciously, thanks to you having shifted yours!

I rest in the knowing that you now understand the Law of Creation and that in the expanded awareness of Hakalau you now see the chicken coup for the illusion it is. You have broken the chains that were deliberately and maliciously placed on The Unicorn that is your birthright, and they will never enslave her again, either in you or your children. Your prosperity is assured. The clues to your future wellbeing were ALL in this book, for those with eyes to see them.

So now, to conclude, a simple exercise. What kind of day will you create for yourself tomorrow? Will it be an absolutely spectacular day or just another groundhog day where nothing changes? It is entirely your decision.

The Motto we were all taught was: "Carpe Diem" = "Seize the Day."

You can now rewrite it and also your future by saying "Seize the Feeling" and your day will take care of itself!

Can you begin each day by quietly stretching your body as you awaken? Then, as you create the feeling you wish to feel all day, energetically reach out to connect with the millions of others of like minded souls who are also reaching out to connect to each other and to you? Can you then breathe quietly for a moment and become aware of their gratitude to you for joining them. Lastly, before rising, can you feel that there are so many more in the circle than there were yesterday? Namaste

Those who do not believe in magic will never find it. For those of us who do?

Game ON . . .

Role of Honour

I do not like the word acknowledgements. I simply wish to create a Role of Honor, a list of the incredible souls who have made great and priceless contributions to my journey. There are hundreds of others who I thank and love and will never forget.

The following list is engraved in gold letters on my heart forever. Please honour them by saying their names aloud just one time. Even the energy of having their names together will vibrate to all who read them.

Larry Czerwonka and all those that worked with him in the production of this book — My thanks for your belief in, and commitment to, humanity!

Berangere Toulet — whose gifted artistry created the magnificent cover for this manuscript.

Jane K. Wardlaw — my guardian angel in this lifetime and the modest and unsung power behind my work. A true Celtic Hearth-mother with a deep love of humanity.

John F Barnes P.T. — my gifted mentor and old soul friend, a tireless traveller who brings the magical healing of myofascial release to me and to the Western world.

Mary Felling P.T. — an incredibly gifted therapist and healer in St. Louis, Missouri, a powerful, formidable spiritual being, yet a compassionate and nurturing woman. A true spiritual old friend and inspiration to myself and many others.

Clay Miller — a true Arizona shaman and trusted old friend, always there, holding space for humanity.

Lara Michelle — friend, healer, in Sedona, an angel in my life guiding me through my darkest night.

Kanoa Okalani — a gifted healer and old friend, from Honolulu, striving to help heal a nation.

Dr. Martina Goldberg — a good friend and an inspirationally tireless worker for humanity in Mexico.

Papa K — a true Hawaiian Legend, from Big Island, mentor and friend. Your spirit lives on in your people.

Simone Awinha — singer, sound healer, and true friend in Holland who believed in me and my work.

Ed Middleton P.T. — a good man and a good and old friend and colleague in Calgary, Canada, a sparkling gift to the world of all who encounter him.

Clarita Schiratti — a young soul full of light in Bariloche, Argentina.

James Twyman — The Peace Troubador, from Oregon, my mentor and a light to the world.

Elyse Hope-Killoran — her magical ways of thinking has helped me and tens of thousands to grow in abundance.

Hermann Muller — from Australia, learning his work in psychosomatic therapy helped me in many ways as it does for thousands.

Kelly Bush-Wilson — from Dallas, Texas, the most highly skilled therapist I have ever met, a true star amongst stars and a good friend.

Odin Aragon — an instant friend when we met, he became like a son to me, he sails the world in racing yachts across the Pacific from USA to Hawaii, flies hot air balloons over the jungle as a business in Mexico, and lives life to the max, always coming from his heart.

Leslie Demytruk R.N. — a loving soul and good friend who opened her heart as a friend and her home to me when I was in need.

Ian Sinclair — a keeper of Scotland's ancient secrets and a strong friend always.

Rebecca Avery — my Celtic/Hawaiian soul sister and friend. A strong, compassionate light to the world from Big Island offering wisdom and love to humanity.

Robert Yarr — a man with a deep vision of a better world who introduced me to many contacts when I returned to my native Scotland.

Jennie Krasse — a friend who truly believes in my work and works tirelessly helping others throughout Maine, USA.

Connor Gilbert — a small flashing light in an ultrasound who one day was gone.

May the combined energies of this list activate the magic of your own potential within you, as it has done for me.

About the Author

Hugh is a globally recognized leader in the field of physical rehabilitation. His groundbreaking and stunningly successful protocol Kinetic Chain Release (KCR) is now being practiced in USA, Canada, Scotland, England, Mexico, Sweden, Iceland, Slovakia, Slovenia, India, Phillipines, Spain, Hawaii, and Argentina (for further info go to www.kineticchainrelease.com) he avoids the much offered title of healer as he feels that adds an unnecessary air of mystery and exclusivity which are egotistic and unnecessary, as the real truth is that everyone is capable of achieving what he has done and much more, if they would only believe in that truth. He therefore provides practical reasons and methodologies showing us all that this is indeed true.

He is a Physical Therapist, Consultant, Author, Lecturer, Researcher, Visionary, Ordained Minister of Spiritual Peacemaking specialising in conflict resolution, and a Qualified Instructor in Dr.Emoto's work with the study of changing the consistency and vibration of water, known as Hado. Hugh has studied and followed the paths of the Native Americans, Celts and Hawaiians and is ever open to receiving more knowledge from these peoples. He became a student of the Knight Templar and is highly respected within that organisation.

He still owns a physical therapy clinic in Calgary Canada, while also developing facilities in U.K. and U.S.A. Hugh and his partner Jane spend much of their time now living in his native Scotland and his other love, Big Island, Hawaii.

He has always been a spokesman for today's youth and works tirelessly to provide them with help in any way possible wherever he travels.

Hugh says he has written this book so that all of the tools that he has found in his journeying through this life are compiled and made available to those who would seek them.

http://www.kineticchainrelease.com

Printed in Great Britain
by Amazon